Learn Chess Tactics

John Nunn

First published in the UK by Gambit Publications Ltd 2004
Reprinted 2006, 2010, 2011, 2015, 2018, 2021, 2023 (2)

ISBN-13: 978-1-901983-98-2
ISBN-10: 1-901983-98-6

DISTRIBUTION:
Worldwide (except USA): Central Books Ltd, 50 Freshwater Road, Chadwell Heath, London RM8 1RX, England.
Tel +44 (0)20 8986 4854 Fax +44 (0)20 8533 5821. E-mail: orders@Centralbooks.com

Gambit Publications Ltd, 27 Queens Pine, Bracknell, Berks, RG12 0TL, England.
E-mail: info@gambitbooks.com
Website (regularly updated): www.gambitbooks.com

Edited by Graham Burgess
Typeset by John Nunn
Printed in the USA by Sheridan MN, Brainerd, Minnesota

10 9

Gambit Publications Ltd
Directors: Dr John Nunn GM, Murray Chandler GM and Graham Burgess FM
German Editor: Petra Nunn WFM
Bookkeeper: Andrea Burgess

Contents

Introduction

This book aims to provide a basic course in chess tactics. We will define a **tactic** to be a short-term operation, using forcing moves, which aims for an immediate concrete gain (such as winning material or mate). Most chess games are decided by tactics. At higher levels, long-term strategic thinking is also important, but even amongst grandmasters tactics predominate. Those who enjoy rapid or blitz chess will already be aware that the faster the time-limit, the more the balance shifts towards tactics. At lower levels, tactics are especially prevalent and the quickest way for most players to achieve better results is to improve their tactical ability.

Learn Chess Tactics is essentially practical in nature, with little in the way of theoretical discussion. The first five chapters deal with the most important and fundamental game-winning tactics: fork, discovered attack, pin, skewer and deflection. The following seven chapters cover slightly more advanced topics. Chapter 13 deals specifically with the way in which the basic tactical elements can be linked together to form more elaborate 'combinations'.

Readers should note that this is not a book about attacking play; the basic ideas presented are those that win material, which is the key to scoring the maximum number of points. Thus you will not find standard attacking combinations (e.g., the bishop sacrifice on h7 or the double bishop sacrifice) in this book. There is in any case little point in covering attacking combinations without a lengthy discussion of attacking play in general; you are unlikely to arrive at a position in which a double bishop sacrifice is possible unless you have aimed for it from an earlier stage. In real life, some games are decided by a direct attack on the enemy king, but far more are won by gaining material.

The structure of each chapter is the same; there is a discussion of the key ideas, with examples, and then there is a set of exercises for the reader to solve. Within each chapter, the exercises are of graduated difficulty, starting with very simple examples and working on to more complex cases. The reader is strongly advised to start at Chapter 1 and work steadily through the book, tackling the exercises at the end of each chapter before moving on to the next one. The reason for this is that later chapters use concepts developed in earlier ones; moreover, the exercises themselves contain important ideas and are not there just for testing whether the reader has been paying attention. There is also a gradual increase in difficulty throughout the book and in later chapters some points are presumed rather than being spelt out in detail as in the earlier chapters. The final chapter consists of a set of exercises in which no hint is given as to theme or difficulty. These present the reader with a situation similar to that of an over-the-board game; the main difference, which can hardly be avoided, is that in a game you don't know whether there really is something to be found.

The positions are all from real games and all except one are from recent (since 1990) play. There are good reasons for this. Positions in books on tactics tend to be heavily recycled, with the result that a slightly more sophisticated reader may well find that he has seen a good proportion of the positions before. I hope to have avoided this by deliberately steering clear of well-known examples and focusing on positions which are recent enough not to have appeared frequently in print. I have also avoided esoteric examples featuring themes of little practical importance; this book focuses on ideas which occur time and time again and which are bound to arise in readers' games sooner or later.

Readers may be surprised by the fact that in many of the examples, one player resigns after losing a relatively modest amount of material. This is a reflection of the fact that most of the examples are taken from games by international players; at this level, losing two pawns (or the equivalent) without compensation is usually a cause for resignation. Even the loss of one pawn, if it is accompanied by a positional disadvantage, may be enough for a player to throw in the towel. Of course, at lower levels the game would normally continue after the loss of material, but being a pawn or two up is bound to give you a head start! This leads on to another point. It would have been easy to include only tactics leading to a large gain of material, but this would create a deceptive impression. Many games are decided by tactics that win a mere pawn (or its equivalent). Having secured a material advantage, the player resolutely swaps all the pieces off, promotes a pawn and finally delivers mate with the extra queen (if the opponent doesn't resign first). I have therefore included some examples in which the gain of material is quite modest.

Some chess knowledge is assumed, but I have provided a quick revision course in the following chapter. Readers may like to have a quick look at this to see if there is any unfamiliar material before proceeding to the main part of the book. Those who have read my earlier book *Learn Chess* will be able to skip this preliminary chapter.

Prerequisites and Symbols

The rules of the game are assumed and will not be covered in this book. The other main prerequisite is a knowledge of chess notation. In this book we use **algebraic notation**, which is the world-wide standard for chess notation.

Notation

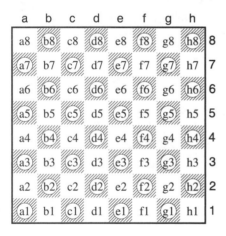

Each of the 64 squares on the chessboard is given a unique name, as shown in the above diagram. The names are based on a system of coordinates, with the left to right direction being represented by the letters 'a' to 'h' and the bottom to top direction being represented by the numbers '1' to '8'.

These names remain the same no matter which side of the board you are looking from, so if you are White then 'a1' will be near you on the left, while if you are Black then 'a1' will be situated on the far side of the board.

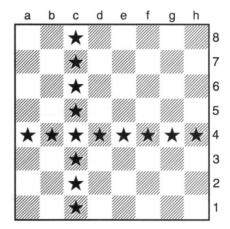

The vertical and horizontal lines of squares on the chessboard are given special names. The vertical columns of squares are called **files**, and the horizontal rows are called **ranks**. In the above diagram one rank and one file have been marked. If you compare this diagram with the previous one, you will see that the squares on the marked file have names running from 'c1' to 'c8' – in other words they all start with a 'c'. For this reason the marked file is called the 'c-file'. The same principle applies to the other seven files. In the same way the eight squares on the marked rank have names running from 'a4' to 'h4'. These all end in a '4', so this is called the fourth rank. Players often refer to ranks from their own perspective, so for White the second rank runs from 'a2' to 'h2', while for Black the second rank runs from 'a7' to 'h7'.

The pieces are represented in this book by figurines, as follows:

King = ♔
Queen = ♕
Rook = ♖

Bishop = ♗
Knight = ♘
Pawn = ♙

Figurines are often used in printed chess notation, as they are independent of language, but for recording games in tournaments players usually use a system of letters which varies from language to language. In English, for example, the letters representing the above sequence are K, Q, R, B, N, P while in German they are K, D, T, L, S, B.

When writing a move in chess notation, first the piece is given and then the destination square. The exception is for pawn moves, when no piece name is used. Thus a knight move to f3 is written '♘f3', while a pawn move to e4 is written simply 'e4'. If a move is a capture then an 'x' is written after the piece name. Pawn captures form an exception, since in this case the original file of the pawn is written. For example, a pawn capture from e3 to d4 is written 'exd4'.

Finally, if a move is a check then '+' is appended to the move, while black moves in isolation are preceded by '...'.

The following diagram shows some chess moves and how they are written.

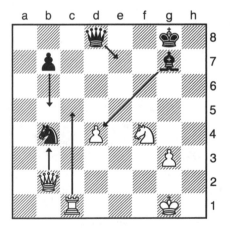

The five marked moves are written: ...b5, ♕xb4, ...♕e7, ...♗xd4+ and ♖c5. You should work out which arrow corresponds to which move. In general, in order to interpret a move written in chess notation, such as '♘e5', you have to find 'e5' on the board, then look for a knight which can move there. If you are not familiar with chess notation this can take some getting used to, but with practice it becomes second nature.

If two pieces of the same type can move to the same square, for example if rooks on a1 and f1 can both move to d1, then the two moves are distinguished by adding the starting file after the piece name (thus either '♖ad1' or '♖fd1' according to which rook moved to d1). If this fails to distinguish the two ambiguous moves, then ranks are used instead: thus if rooks on c1 and c7 can both move to c5, we write either '♖1c5' or '♖7c5' as appropriate. Pawn promotions are written, for example, 'a8♕', meaning that White advanced a pawn to a8 and promoted it to a queen.

The following table summarizes the additional symbols used in the chess notation in this book:

Check	=	+
Double check	=	++
Mate	=	#
Castles kingside	=	0-0
Castles queenside	=	0-0-0
Good move	=	!
Bad move	=	?
Brilliant move	=	!!
Serious mistake	=	??

Moves which are part of a game are generally written with move numbers. For example, here is a very short game which also uses some of the symbols given above: 1 e4 e5 2 ♗c4 ♘c6 3 ♕h5 ♘f6?? 4 ♕xf7#. Note that a white move and its following black move are given the same move number. In this book, we usually join games somewhere in the middle, so the first move given may have almost any move number. The result of a game may be indicated as follows:

1-0	The game ends in a win for White
½-½	The game ends in a draw
0-1	The game ends in a win for Black

Conventions

There are a few other conventions of chess writing which are worth mentioning. The diagonal lines of squares on the chessboard are called simply **diagonals** and the two diagonals from a1 to h8 and h1 to a8 are called **long diagonals**. We refer to a piece on a particular square as, for example, 'the pawn on e4' or 'the e4-pawn'. The players are called **White** and **Black** and are capitalized. Thus we have 'White's bishop' or 'Black's e5-pawn'. However, white and black (without capitals) can also be used as adjectives, referring to the colours of the pieces, as in 'the white bishop' or 'the weak black e-pawn'. On the chessboard there are 32 **light squares** and 32 **dark squares**. If some captures result in the removal of equal amounts of white and black material, we speak of an **exchange**; the simplest case is when one white piece and one black piece of the same type are captured. Rather confusingly, the common material advantage of rook for knight or rook for bishop is referred to as **the exchange**; thus we speak of 'winning the exchange'. It should be clear from the context which meaning of 'exchange' is intended.

In this book we adopt a few additional conventions which are far from universal in chess writing. Firstly, moves given in bold are those actually played in the game. Secondly, some of the diagrams contain arrows indicating points of importance. Solid arrows represent moves actually played, while dotted arrows represent potential moves or threats. A small 'W' or 'B' by the side of the diagram indicates who is to move in the diagram position.

When a game is quoted, we give the names of the players and the event in which the game took place. Often in chess books you will see a variety of abbreviations used to show the type of event in which the game was played. In this book we will usually write event names out in full and use only one abbreviation, namely 'Ch' for 'Championship'.

Material

Chess games are often decided by a **material advantage** – whoever has the larger army is likely to win. It is easy to compare a position in which White has a knight, a bishop and a pawn and Black has a knight and a pawn – clearly White is a bishop up. But who has a material advantage when White has a queen, a bishop and a pawn and Black has two rooks and two pawns? To answer such questions, chess-players have worked out a table of material values for the various pieces:

Pawn   =   1
Knight   =   3
Bishop   =   3
Rook   =   5
Queen   =   9

This table allows one to work out who is ahead on material. In the example given above White has 9+3+1 = 13 while Black has 10+2 = 12, so White is one point (which is equivalent to one pawn) up. The king does not feature in this table because loss of the king ends the game, so its relative value is a meaningless concept. It must be emphasized that this table of material values is a rule of thumb rather than a strict law. A particular position may favour one type of piece over another, and in this case the values need to be modified. As a general principle, **a material advantage of two points is sufficient to win**, subject to certain provisos. First of all, there should be no compensation for the extra material – if there is a mating attack, for example, the material situation is irrelevant. Compensation can take many forms, some quite subtle, but compensation for material loss normally arises when the material is sacrificed deliberately. If it is lost accidentally, then compensation is much less likely to arise, although the player who is about to gain material should always check to see if he is damaging his position in the process. Secondly, the side with the extra material should still have some pawns. The main winning method when material ahead is to exchange pieces and eventually promote a pawn; if you don't have any pawns left, this isn't possible. Finally, this two-point rule assumes accurate play! Of course this raises the question as to whether a one-point advantage is enough to win. Unfortunately, it all depends on the position and there is no general rule which enables one to decide.

We can see how important winning material is, but gaining material is easier said than done. If you attack an enemy piece, your opponent may overlook the threat, but once you get beyond the beginner level this is very unusual. More often he will respond to and nullify your threat. How, then, can you achieve the material gain which is necessary for victory? That is the subject of this book. There are standard tactical devices which win material in thousands of games every day. Being familiar with these will win you plenty of games and save you many more.

1 Fork

In chess, making a single threat often doesn't have any real impact. For example, if you attack a piece, then your opponent may defend it or move it out of range of the attack. Creating two threats simultaneously is a different matter. In many cases, there will be no way to meet both threats and material loss will be inevitable. The **fork** is one of the simplest ways to set up a double threat; the essential idea is that one of your pieces moves to a position where it creates two threats simultaneously. In the most basic version, the two threats are simply attacks against vulnerable enemy pieces.

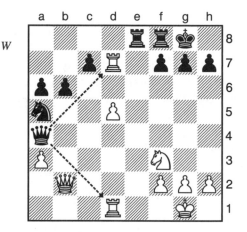

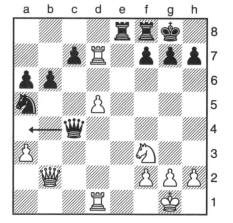

J. Polgar – Macieja
Rapidplay, Budapest 2002

This position is a clear example. Black played **23...♛a4**, attacking both undefended white rooks. The diagram at the top of the next column shows the situation. There is no way for White to defend both rooks, so she resigned at once rather than play on a whole rook down.

Although the fork is one of the most basic tactical devices, it is also one of the most common in practice and decides countless games at all levels of play from beginner up to (as in the above example) grandmaster. It is therefore especially important to gain experience at spotting forks, both in order to execute them yourself and to avoid allowing them by your opponent. Of course, grandmasters don't normally allow a simple fork such as the above – this example is very much the exception – yet even this elementary case reveals an important psychological point. A fork is easier to overlook if there is something a little bit out of the ordinary about it. It is not immediately obvious that the white rooks are vulnerable to a fork; they are only undefended because the pawn on d5 interrupts the communication between them. Moreover, one 'prong' of the fork points up the board and the other points down, which often makes a fork harder to see than if both prongs point forwards into the enemy position. This chapter and the numerous exercises at the end provide plenty of chances for you to gain useful 'fork-spotting' experience.

As with many of the tactical ideas featured in this book, a fork gains in strength if a check is involved.

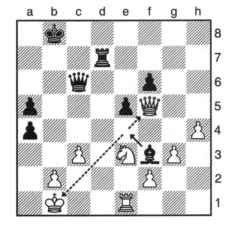

Holmsten – G. Mohr
European Team Ch, Leon 2001

In this position, White had just played his king from c1 to b1; he now resigned without waiting for 33...♗e4+, which wins White's queen in return for a bishop. Forks executed by checking moves are quite common because a check is a very forcing move; the opponent has to respond to the check, which often leaves him little chance to deal with any other threats created by the checking move. It follows that a king exposed to checks is a weakness even if the king cannot be directly attacked. The checks give rise to many possible forks, and avoiding these forks restricts the player's options.

A particularly vulnerable formation is an exposed king together with one or more undefended pieces. In this case an enemy piece can both check the king and attack an undefended piece. The queen is especially effective at exploiting this situation and can do plenty of damage single-handed.

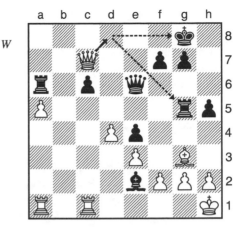

R. Ruck – Krasenkow
European Ch, Ohrid 2001

In this position the black king is exposed to checks along the back rank. White's queen is in a position to check on either b8 or d8, and that means that any undefended pieces which can be attacked from b8 or d8 are liable to be lost to a queen fork. Black's previous move was the unwise advance of his h-pawn from h6 to h5. This left his rook on g5 undefended and White was not slow to take advantage of this by **33 ♕d8+**, both checking the king and attacking the loose rook. Faced with the loss of his rook, Black resigned immediately. Once again there is a psychological element to Black's blunder. He must have realized before playing ...h5 that White's checks on b8 and d8 were not genuinely dangerous, and therefore thought he could use a tempo to start some kingside counterplay by pushing his h-pawn. Unfortunately, it was this very move which transformed ♕d8+ from a harmless check into a deadly game-winner. It is not enough to make sure that your opponent has no tactical threats; you must also ensure that there are no tactical possibilities in the position **after** your intended move.

Forks do not have to involve direct attacks on undefended pieces. Another possibility is that the fork attacks a vulnerable piece and at the same time threatens to deliver mate. Just as with a check, a threat of mate **has** to be dealt with at once and this gives the attacker a free tempo to wreak havoc elsewhere.

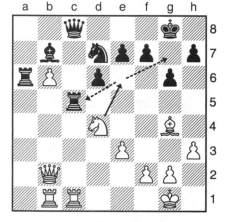

Izeta – Sanz Alonso
Elgoibar 1999

Here there are no undefended pieces to exploit, but nevertheless White found a lethal fork. He played **31 ♘e6**, threatening both 32 ♘xc5 and, more seriously, 32 ♕g7#. Clearly the mate threat takes priority over everything else. Black can meet it with a move such as 31...f6 or 31...♘f6, but then White takes the rook on c5 with a decisive material advantage. Note that Black cannot reply 31...fxe6, because of mate in two by 32 ♗xe6+ ♚f8 33 ♕h8#. Black's only other possibility is 31...♖xc1+, but after 32 ♖xc1 White wins Black's queen, because 33 ♖xc8+ and 33 ♕g7# are both threatened. Therefore Black resigned at once. Although the rook on c5 was protected, it was vulnerable to an attack by a knight because a rook is worth considerably more than a knight. Here Black probably overlooked the decisive knight move because the e6-square was apparently covered by the f7-pawn; White, however, saw further and realized that the knight was invulnerable on e6.

Any piece is capable of delivering a fork, but the two pieces most effective at forking are the queen and the knight. The reason is that the queen and knight can attack in eight directions simultaneously and therefore have better chances of catching enemy pieces in a fork than the rook and bishop, which can only attack in four directions, or the pawn, which is restricted to just two. The king, it is true, can also attack in eight ways, but it is such a short range piece that is not very effective at forking. In addition, the king is normally not in the thick of the battle and therefore usually only comes within range of the enemy in the endgame, when there isn't much around to fork.

Both the queen and knight can create forks which are relatively hard to spot in advance. In the queen's case, this is because its long-range action is capable of forking pieces at opposite ends of the board (as in the first example above, J.Polgar-Macieja) so that no undefended piece is safe. In the knight's case, its crooked mode of action makes a fork that little bit less visible.

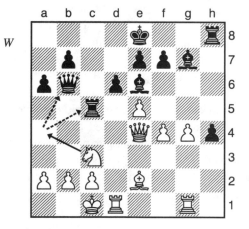

Ponomariov – V. Milov
European Ch, Ohrid 2001

Black has just played his rook from c8 to c5. This turned out to be a mistake because White replied **22 ♘a4**, attacking the rook and queen simultaneously. Black had no choice but to deal with the threat to the more valuable queen, leaving the knight to take the rook. Winning the **exchange** (rook for knight or rook for bishop) without compensation almost always confers a decisive advantage, but here Black had the additional misfortune that White was able to break through quickly in the centre. The finish was **22...♕a5 23 ♘xc5 ♕xc5 24 f5 ♗xa2 25 f6 ♗f8 26 ♕a4+** (a further fork of king and bishop) **26...b5 27 ♕xa2 ♕e3+ 28 ♔b1 1-0**. It is possible that Black thought he could counter White's knight fork by 22...♕c6, attacking the white queen, only to realize too late that White wins the exchange in any case by playing 23 ♘xc5, because this capture also defends the queen.

It is of course pleasant when you get the chance to play a simple fork as in the examples above, but few opponents are so cooperative. More often there is no immediate fork, but it is possible to force the opponent's pieces into position for a subsequent fork. Sometimes this preliminary action involves no more than a check to drive the enemy king onto the right square, as in the following example.

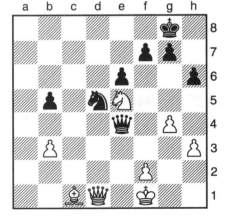

Soppe – Braga
Villa Gisell 1998

In this position White had just played his knight from f3 to e5, taking a black bishop in the process. As White is now a piece up, he no doubt expected that Black would recapture the knight on e5. However, Black saw that the opening of the queen's line from e4-h1 gave him the opportunity to set up a fork by means of a check. He played **40...♕h1+** and White resigned since after 41 ♔e2 ♘c3+ his king and queen would be forked and he would face disastrous loss of material. It is a mistake to assume that just because you have made a capture, your opponent must recapture.

In the following example, two preliminary checks are needed to line Black's king up for the decisive fork.

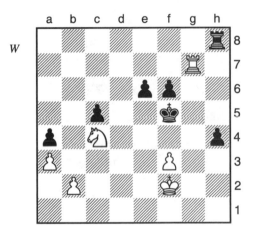

Bareev – Onishchuk
Rapidplay, Moscow 2002

In this position White has the material advantage of a knight for two pawns, and would probably have won in the end in any case, but he saw the chance to finish the game at a stroke. He continued **45 ♘d6+** and Black resigned. There are two possibilities. If Black plays 45...♔e5, then 46 ♘f7+ forks the king and rook. The alternative is 45...♔f4, but then 46 ♖g4+ drives the king to e5 in any case, and after 46...♔e5 47 ♘f7+ Black again loses his rook for nothing. It is interesting to note that Black's previous move was to advance his pawn from h5 to h4. Previously White's check on d6 was not a serious threat, but by pushing the pawn Black allowed White an additional check on g4, and this proved his undoing.

In the opening phase of the game, it isn't unusual for the traditional weakness of the f7-square (or f2-square if White is the victim) to play a part in a forking combination.

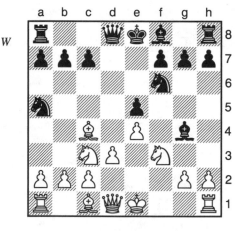

Mirumian – Stehlik
Plzen 2000

The above position arose after the opening moves **1 e4 e5 2 ♘c3 d6 3 ♗c4 ♘f6 4 d3 ♘c6 5 f4 ♗g4 6 ♘f3 ♘a5 7 fxe5 dxe5?** (7...♗xf3 is correct). White saw the opportunity for a fork on e5 and continued **8 ♗xf7+! ♔xf7** (8...♔e7 is no better as Black loses both a pawn and the right to castle) **9 ♘xe5+** (the fork arrives and White ends up two pawns ahead) **9...♔g8 10 ♘xg4 ♘xg4 11 ♕xg4 h5?** (the position is lost in any case, but this further error, losing the a5-knight to a queen fork, cuts the game short) **12 ♕e6+ ♔h7 13 ♕f5+ g6 14 ♕xa5 1-0**.

Checking isn't the only way to set up a future fork. Another possibility is to clear the square on which the fork will take place.

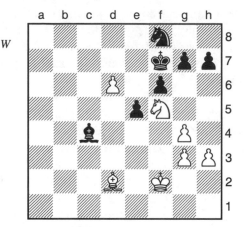

Shirov – Topalov
Rapidplay, Prague 2002

This position can be solved by the 'if only' method. We first have to spot that there is a potential knight fork of Black's king and bishop on d6. Indeed, White's knight is already poised on a square from which it can jump to d6, so White would have an immediate win, 'if only' his pawn were not blocking the crucial square. The question then is how White can get rid of the obstructive pawn and make his wish come true. White continued **40 d7!**, threatening to promote the pawn. Black has to deal with this threat, which would give White an extra queen, but then White has time to execute his knight fork. The finish was **40...♘xd7 41 ♘d6+ ♔g6 42 ♘xc4 h5** (Black has only one pawn for the piece, so White is sure to win provided he takes a little care; in particular, he must retain at least one pawn) **43 gxh5+ ♔xh5 44 ♘d6 ♔g6 45 g4 ♘b6 46 ♔f3 ♘d5 47 ♔e4 ♘c7 48 ♘f5 ♔f7 49 h4 g6 50 ♘h6+ ♔e6 51 h5 gxh5 52 gxh5 1-0**.

One of the most common methods of setting up a fork is by means of a sacrifice. Forcing sacrifices based on checks or captures often have to be accepted, setting the stage for the follow-up which regains all the sacrificed material and more.

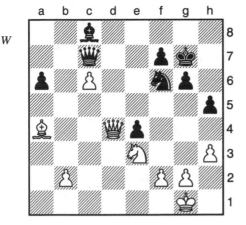

de Firmian – P. Carlsson
Stockholm 2002

Almeida – Abreu
Cuban Ch, Holguin City 2002

Black's knight on f6 is **pinned** by the white queen, since it cannot legally move. Therefore one might be tempted to play 38 ♘d5, which forks the black queen and the pinned knight. However, not all forks are decisive and here Black can reply 38...♕d6, moving one attacked piece and at the same time defending the other. However, we are on the right lines with the idea of a fork on d5, but it has to be set up the correct way. White played **38 ♕xf6+!** and Black resigned. Black must recapture on f6 or else he will be a piece down, but after 38...♔xf6 39 ♘d5+ followed by 40 ♘xc7 White emerges a piece ahead in any case. As mentioned in the introduction, it is often hard to separate one tactical element from another, and all but the simplest pieces of tactics usually involve more than one of the basic tactical ideas. Here White's queen sacrifice was a **deflection**, drawing the enemy king onto the correct square for the knight fork. We shall have more to say about deflections in Chapter 5.

In the above case the preliminary sacrifice was a capture, so Black had to accept or else remain material down. It is often harder to see preliminary sacrifices which do not involve a capture (so-called **empty-square sacrifices**), but they can be just as effective.

A potential fork exists on f6, but first White must deflect the black king to a suitable square. The game continued **26 ♖h7+!** and Black resigned. If Black accepts the sacrifice by 26...♔xh7 then 27 ♘xf6+ forks his king and queen; the upshot is that White wins a queen for a rook. However, declining the sacrifice is no better as the king cannot continue to guard the bishop; after 26...♔f8 27 ♘xf6 White not only wins the bishop, but also picks up further material because he is now forking Black's queen and rook.

Another common preliminary idea is that of **removing the guard**. Once again, we shall look at this in more detail later (Chapter 7), but the principle is that a fork would be possible, except that an enemy piece is covering the square on which the fork is to be executed. A preliminary sacrifice may be needed to eliminate or deflect the piece that is preventing the fork.

In the diagram overleaf, there is a possible knight fork on f3, but at the moment it is prevented by the white pawn on g2. How can Black remove this pawn so as to execute his fork? The game continued **42...♘h3+!** and White resigned. He cannot decline the sacrifice since 43 ♔h1 allows immediate mate by

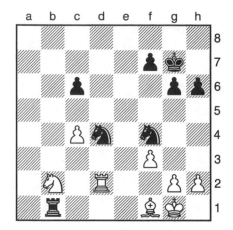

Ionescu – Aronian
Bucharest 1999

43...♖xf1#. However, accepting it by 43 gxh3 removes the pawn's guard of f3, and after 43...♘xf3+ 44 ♔f2 ♘xd2 White loses not only rook for knight, but even a further piece as he cannot save both bishop and knight.

As with all the tactical ideas in this book, when they occur in isolation they are not so difficult to spot, but they can be put together in combinations of almost limitless complexity. We will take a look at a more complex example to show some of the possibilities.

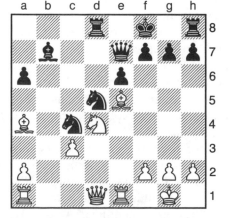

Kramnik – Karpov
Rapidplay, Frankfurt 1999

It isn't obvious that the decisive point of White's attack will be a queen fork from the square e2! White continued **20 ♗xg7+!**, in itself a fork of Black's king and h8-rook. Black was forced to accept or lose the exchange and a pawn, but after **20...♔xg7** came **21 ♘f5+** forking king and queen. Here White is using the **pin** along the e-file to justify his play. Moving the king is no help, as White would then win queen and pawn for bishop and knight (a gain of four points), so Black played **21...exf5 22 ♖xe7 ♘xe7** (*see next diagram*).

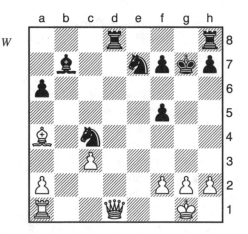

A quick count shows that Black has a rook and two knights for a queen and a pawn, so he is actually one point ahead on material. Has all White's brilliance been in vain? No, because White now played **23 ♕e2**, forking the two enemy knights. Black is unable to save them both and so, instead of being one point up, he will be two points down, almost always a decisive disadvantage. The game concluded in an easy win for White: **23...♘g6 24 ♕xc4 ♖d2 25 ♗b3 ♗d5 26 ♕xa6 ♖d8 27 ♗xd5 ♖8xd5 28 h3 ♘e5 29 a4 f4 30 a5 f3 31 ♕b7 fxg2 32 a6 1-0**. White needed considerable foresight to spot the final ♕e2 before embarking on the initial sacrifice. Such an elaborate combination, involving three forks, may not come easily at first because although the building blocks are not too difficult in themselves, the art of assembling them into a complete combination can only be acquired with practice.

Fork Exercises

Solutions start on page 111.

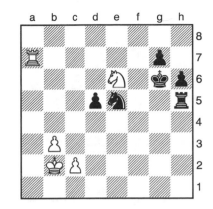

3
W

How did White force immediate resignation?

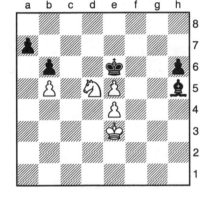

1
W

How did White win material and the game?

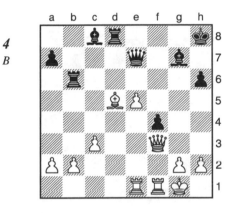

4
B

Material is roughly equal. What should Black play?

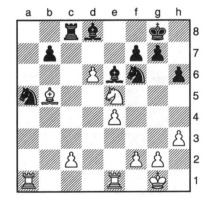

2
B

White has just taken a pawn on e5 with his knight. Was this a good idea?

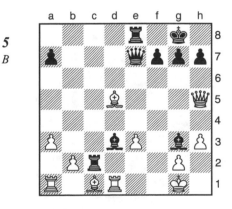

5
B

How did Black win the game with a fork?

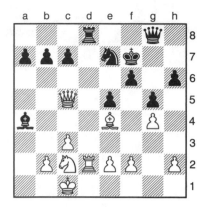

6 W

How did White use a fork to win a piece?

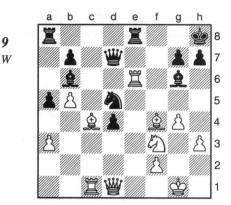

9 W

How does White win a piece with a fork?

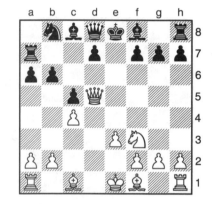

7 B

Black has just moved his rook from a8 to a7. Was this a good idea?

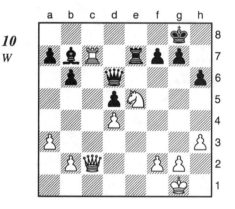

10 W

A sharp tactic netted White a piece. How?

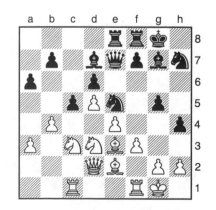

8 B

How did Black use a fork to win the game at once?

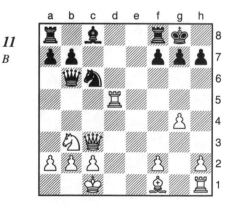

11 B

How can Black win material with a knight fork?

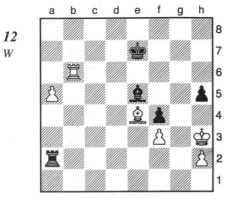

12
W

How did White win material in this world championship match game?

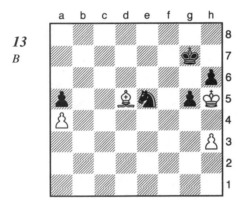

13
B

How did Black finish the game at a stroke?

14
B

How did Black win a piece?

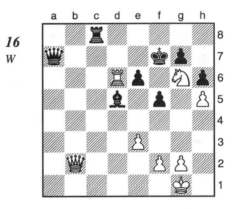

15
B

What should Black do about his attacked queen?

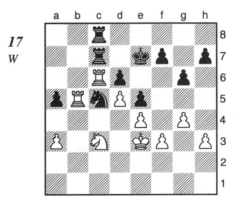

16
W

How can White win the black queen?

17
W

How did White win a piece?

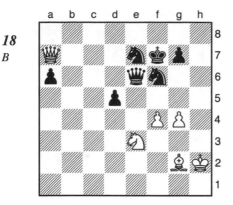

18
B

How did Black finish the game straight away?

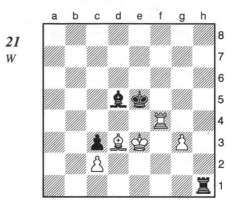

21
W

How did White win a piece?

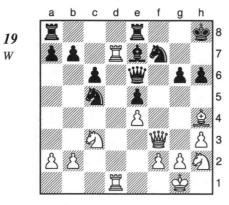

19
W

White is able to win a piece. How?

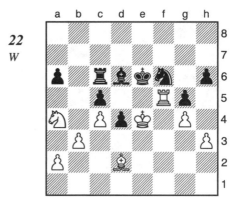

22
W

White is in check. What should he play?

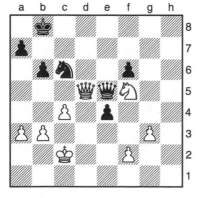

20
B

How can Black force a win?

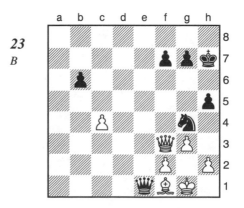

23
B

How did Black win a vital pawn?

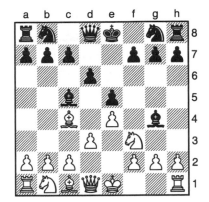

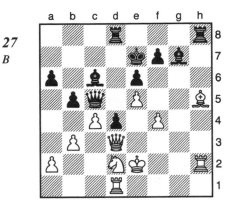

Here White played **5 ♗xf7+**. Does this win material?

How does Black use the undefended rook on h2 to win material?

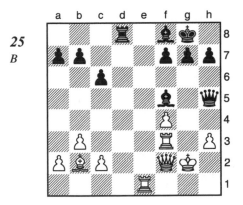

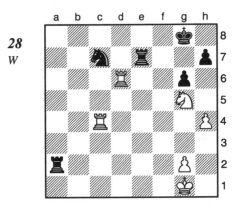

How did Black win the exchange using a fork?

How did White set up a decisive knight fork?

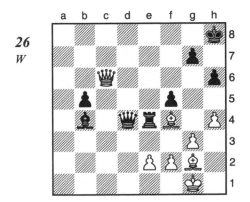

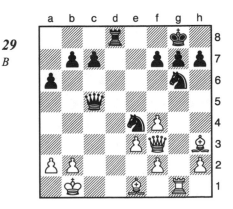

Does White have anything better than 32 ♗xe4 followed by 33 ♕xb5, winning a pawn?

How did Black use a fork to launch a mating attack?

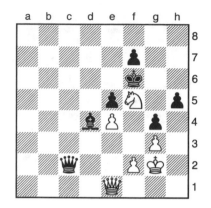

30
B

The position looks hard to win but Black made it seem easy. How?

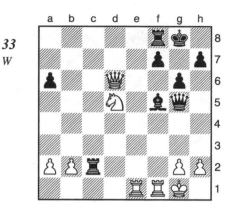

33
W

Black threatens mate in one on g2. How should White react?

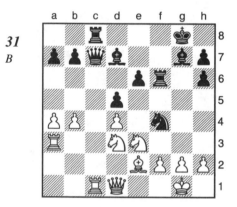

31
B

Black's queen is attacked. What should he do?

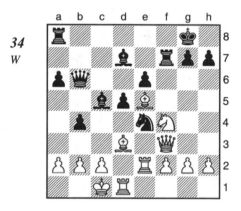

34
W

How does White set up a decisive fork?

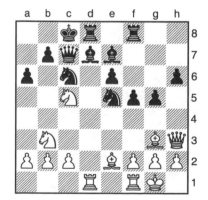

32
W

How did White use a fork to win two pawns?

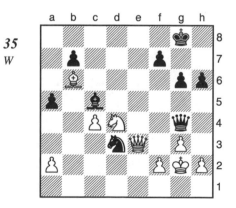

35
W

How did White win a piece?

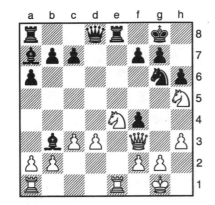

36
W

Black has just taken a piece on b3. Should White recapture?

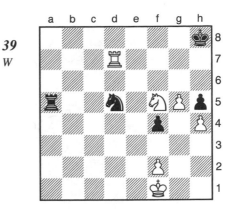

39
W

How can White win a piece with a knight fork?

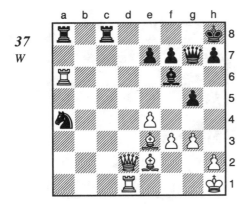

37
W

A slightly unusual fork netted White a piece. How?

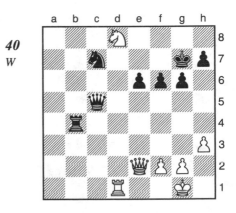

40
W

How did White use a knight fork to launch a deadly attack?

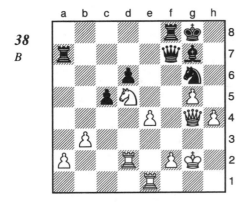

38
B

How did Black win material by a spectacular combination?

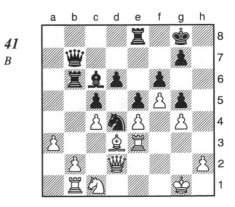

41
B

How did Black win a vital pawn?

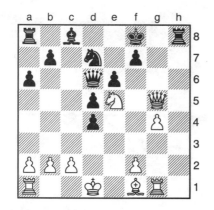

42
W

How does White win using a knight fork?

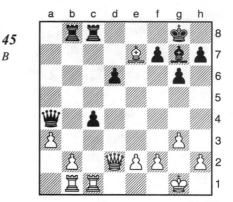

45
B

How did Black set up a decisive queen fork?

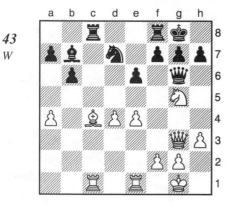

43
W

How can White win at least one pawn?

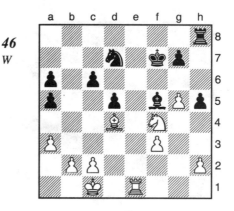

46
W

How did White set up a knight fork with two preliminary sacrifices?

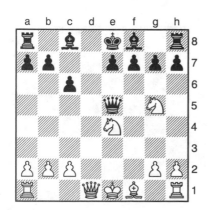

44
B

Should Black regain the sacrificed piece with 11...f6 or 11...h6?

2 Discovered Attack

Like the fork (see Chapter 1), the **discovered attack** is a way of creating two threats at the same time. Unlike the fork, the discovered attack involves **two** attacking pieces. The following diagram shows the basic idea.

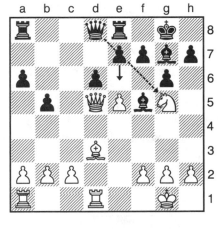

Grubisić – Tischendorf
Darmstadt 1993

White has an undefended knight on g5, which is on the same diagonal as Black's queen. At the moment there is a black pawn in the way, but Black now played **16...e6**. This moves the pawn out of the way, discovering an attack by the black queen on White's knight. At the same time the pawn itself attacks the white queen. Thus Black has created two threats, one directly and one by discovery. White's queen cannot move so as to defend the knight, and so White loses a piece. In the game White struggled on for a few moves before resigning.

In a discovered attack, we call the piece which actually moves the **firing piece** and the piece which has its line of attack opened the **rear piece**. In the above example the e7-pawn is the firing piece and the black queen is the rear piece. The rear piece in a discovered attack is always a line-moving piece (rook, bishop or queen) but the firing piece can be anything.

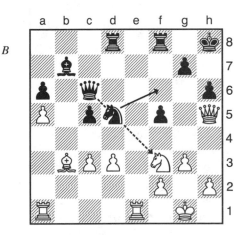

Z. Almasi – Adams
European Team Ch, Pula 1997

Here's another example. Black's queen and bishop are lined up on the long diagonal, and Black would be able to take the white knight on f3 if only his own d5-knight were not in the way. Any move by this knight will threaten to win a piece by ...♕xf3, but White can meet this single threat by, for example, ♖e3. Therefore Black must look for a way to move the d5-knight so as to set up a second threat. The move **27...♘f6** fits the bill admirably. In addition to the threat to the f3-knight, Black directly attacks White's queen. White cannot cope with both threats and must lose a piece; he therefore resigned immediately.

A discovered attack may not exist immediately, but can be prepared by a suitable sequence of forcing moves.

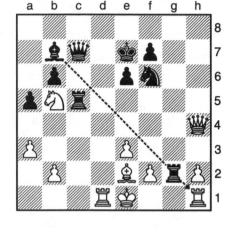

Portisch – Karpov
Biel 1996

In this position there is a potential discovered attack along the long diagonal. White has an undefended rook on h1 which would be under threat if the rook on g2 moved away. However, there is no immediate discovered attack and, moreover, Black must first deal with the attack on his queen. Karpov solved the problem by **18...♖xb5!**. This preliminary sacrifice not only eliminates the attack on the queen, but also deflects the white bishop away from e2, and so allows Black to play his rook to g4. The finish was **19 ♗xb5 ♖g4** and White resigned because he must now move his queen, whereupon he loses a whole rook on h1. Taking into account the initial sacrifice on b5, the net result is that Black has won a piece.

A check is one of the most forcing moves, so a discovered attack which is also a check gives the defender less chance to escape from his predicament. Either of the two pieces involved in a discovered attack can deliver check. In the next position it is the firing piece which checks.

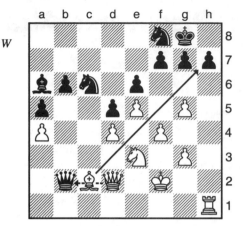

Rašik – Isonzo
Mitropa Cup, Leipzig 2002

In this position the two queens are lined up, with only a white bishop separating them. The game ended **32 ♗xh7+** and Black resigned, since he has to deal with the check, whereupon White can safely take Black's queen.

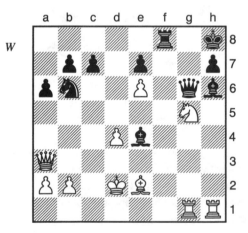

Karpov – Leko
Tilburg 1996

This is a more complex example because a preliminary sacrifice is necessary to set up the discovered attack. In the diagram White is marginally ahead on material (rook for bishop and pawn), but his h1-rook is under attack and his g5-knight is caught in a nasty pin. White turned the tables by **28 ♖xh6! ♛xh6 29 ♛e3**; suddenly Black's bishop is under attack and he also faces the threat of 30 ♘f7+ with a discovered attack against Black's queen. The result is that Black will end up at least a piece down, and he therefore resigned. This particular combination was hard to see because the line-up which is characteristic of a discovered attack did not exist in the diagram, but had to be set up by the correct sequence of moves.

If the rear piece of a discovered attack delivers check, then we speak of a **discovered check**. This type of discovered attack is particularly strong because the firing piece has virtually complete freedom to move where it wants. The rear piece delivers check, which the defender has to deal with. The firing piece then gets **another** move before the defender gets a chance to respond. With two free moves to play with, it is not surprising that quite a lot of damage can be done.

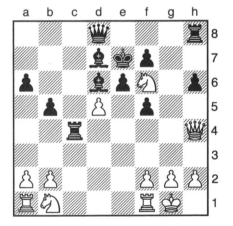

Zifroni – Manor
Czerniak memorial,
Bikurei Haitim/Tel Aviv 1997

This is a typical example. White's queen and knight are lined up against the enemy king. Any move by the knight will deliver check by discovery from White's queen. However, White has to take into account the attack on his queen from the c4-rook. The multi-purpose discovered check **17 ♘e4+** both blocks the fourth rank and prepares to take the bishop on d6. Black will lose his queen, for example 17...♔f8 18 ♛xd8+ or 17...♔e8 18 ♘xd6+ ♔f8 19 ♛xd8+, and he therefore resigned.

Discovered checks are so powerful that it is often worth a considerable sacrifice to set one up.

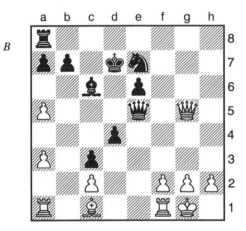

Rogulj – Atlas
Zonal tournament, Dresden 1998

Black is well down on material (rook and pawn for knight) but White's king lacks defenders. Black managed to break through with a brilliant combination based on sacrificing his queen to set up a lethal discovered check. The game continued **18...♖g8!!** (attacking the white queen and setting up an attack against g2) **19 ♛xe5** (White may as well take the queen) **19...♖xg2+ 20 ♔h1** (now the discovered check has been set up; Black would like to mate by playing his rook along the g-file, but first he must remove the f2-pawn to prevent White from blocking the long diagonal with f3) **20...♖xf2+** (this example demonstrates the key feature of the discovered check with brutal clarity; the defender has to respond to the check from the rear piece, so the firing piece can wreak havoc with impunity) **21 ⌾g1 ♖g2+ 22 ⌾h1** (the king must return to the corner, allowing a second and final discovered check) **22...♖g3+** and White resigned since it is mate in two more moves.

The discovered check may seem deadly enough, but it is not the ultimate chess weapon. That accolade belongs to the **double check**, a special type of discovered check in which the firing piece and the rear piece both check the enemy king simultaneously. The key feature of the double check is that the **only legal reply is a king move**. Most double checks form part of a mating attack, but the following example shows that other motivations are possible.

![Golod – Zak chess diagram, White to move]

Golod – Zak
Israeli Team Ch 2002

Here White is a piece up, but his knight is under attack and if the knight moves then Black can promote his pawn. White played **31 ♘xf5!**, apparently allowing the pawn to advance. However, if Black plays 31...d1♕ then White replies with the double check 32 ♘d6++. A double check forces a king move,

and then White can safely play 33 ♖xd1 because the double check has blocked the d-file with gain of tempo and thus left Black's queen undefended. Note that 32 ♘e3+ is bad, because this is merely a discovered check, and so Black can reply 32...♕xf1+, remaining material up in the endgame. The game actually finished **31...♖d3 32 ♘d6++ ⌾e6 33 ♖d1 1-0**.

There is one type of discovered attack which is very easy to overlook. This involves what we call **pin-breaking**. The following example makes the idea clear.

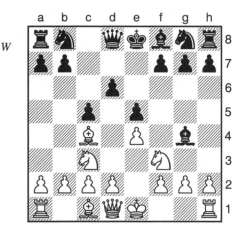

Conde Rodriguez – Munoz Palmerin
Vila de Padron 2000

This position arose after the moves **1 e4 e5 2 ♘f3 d6 3 ♗c4 ♗g4 4 ♘c3 c5?**. Black's g4-bishop is apparently pinning the white knight on f3. Indeed, if the knight moves then Black can take White's queen. You may recall that it is sometimes possible to win material with a forking combination based on ♗xf7+ (see page 14), but it doesn't work here since after 5 ♗xf7+? ⌾xf7 6 ♘xe5+ dxe5 7 ♕xg4 White has lost a piece. Nevertheless, White does have a way to win material based on the weakness of f7. This depends on the fact that a pin against any piece other than a king is not absolute; the pinned piece can still legally move, and if it can create a strong enough threat then the pin may turn out to be a **discovered attack for the other side**. White now played **5 ♘xe5!**. This threatens 6 ♗xf7+ ♔e7 7 ♘d5#, which is such a strong threat that the fact that White's queen can be taken is irrelevant. Black could have played on a pawn down by 5...dxe5 6 ♕xg4 ♘c6, but he decided to allow the mate: **5...♗xd1 6 ♗xf7+ ♔e7 7 ♘d5#**.

The use of pin-breaking to convert a pin into a discovered attack often proves totally unexpected to the opponent, and it is surprising how often it occurs in practice.

In the following example, it was not a mate threat but a threat to the enemy queen which allowed the pin to be broken.

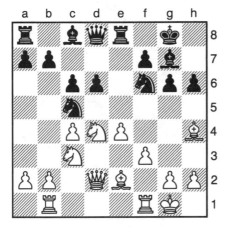

Stone – Nijboer
Den Bosch 1999

Here the knight on f6 appears pinned, but Black broke the pin by **13...♘fxe4!**. The pin has been converted into a discovered attack, with the knight attacking White's queen, and the black queen attacking White's h4-bishop. With so many pieces under attack, it is necessary to calculate all the variations carefully, but it is not too difficult: after 14 ♗xd8 ♘xd2 White is not only a pawn down, but has four pieces under attack; 14 fxe4 ♕xh4 leaves

Black a pawn up with a large positional advantage because the e4-pawn is very weak; finally, 14 ♘xe4 ♕xh4 also gives Black an extra pawn which White cannot regain by 15 ♘xd6 because then his d4-knight can be captured. After 13...♘fxe4!, White did not care to play on a pawn down with a bad position, and he immediately resigned.

Discovered Attack Exercises

Solutions start on page 117.

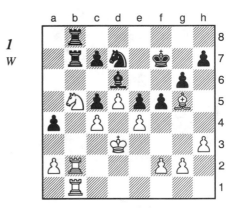

How did White win using a discovered attack?

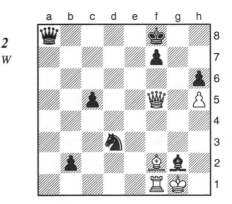

A discovered attack wins quickly. How?

3
B

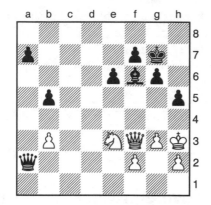

Black, two pawns up, decided to grab a third by **41...♕xb3**. Was this a good idea?

6
B

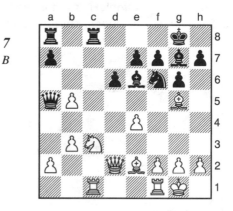

How did Black win with a discovered attack?

4
B

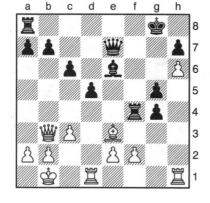

Black's rook is under attack. Does he have to move it?

7
B

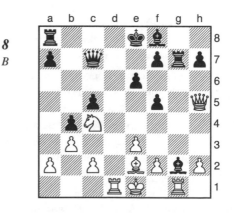

Here Black played **14...♖xc3 15 ♖xc3 ♘xe4**, forking queen, rook and bishop. Was this a good idea?

5
W

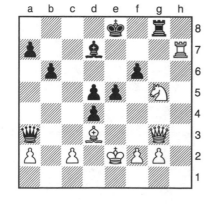

What is the simplest way for White to win?

8
B

Black won with a discovered attack. How?

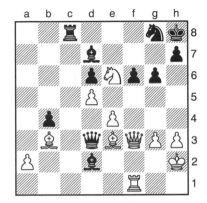

9 W

A discovered attack decides the game. How?

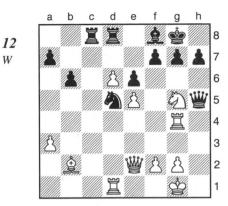

12 W

How did White set up a discovered attack with a preliminary sacrifice?

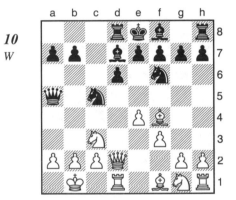

10 W

The line-up of queens on d2 and a5 suggests a discovered attack. Is there one here?

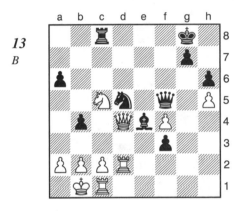

13 B

How did Black win material by a discovered attack?

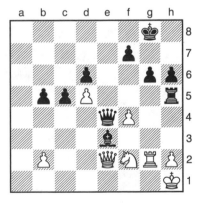

11 B

How did Black finish the game at a stroke?

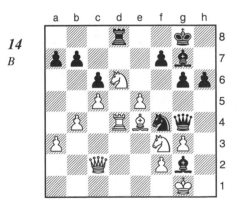

14 B

In this rather complex position, how can Black win material?

15
B

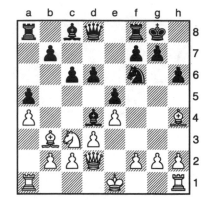

How did Black win a pawn?

18
B

How did a discovered check help Black to win?

16
B

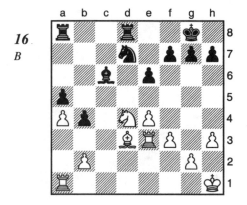

Black's bishop is attacked. What is his best continuation?

19
B

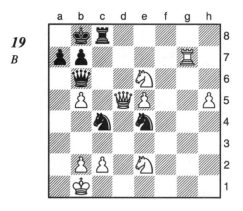

How did Black set up a decisive discovered check?

17
W

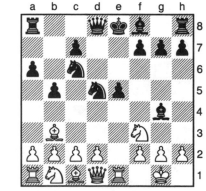

White won quickly. How?

20
W

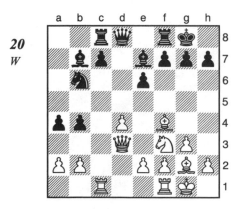

How did White win an important pawn?

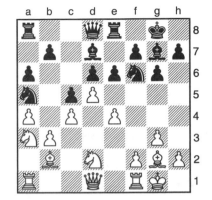

21
B

How did Black win a pawn with a discovered attack?

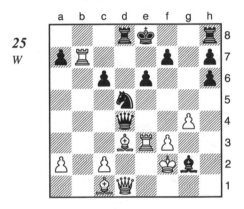

24
W

What is the quickest win for White?

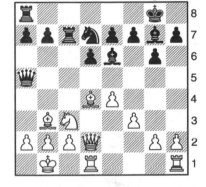

22
W

How did White win a pawn?

25
W

How did White win material with a surprising discovered attack?

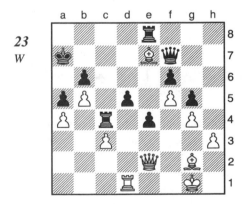

23
W

How did White win material by arranging a discovered attack?

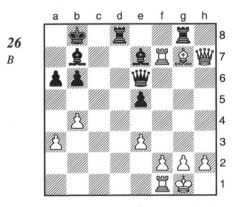

26
B

Black played **26...♛xf7**. Was this a good move?

3 Pin

The pin is one of the most basic tactics, but it has immense practical importance. It is very easy, even for masters and grandmasters, to overlook the effect of a pin and thereby lose material. The basic idea involves three pieces, one friendly and two enemy, all lying on the same line. Here is an example.

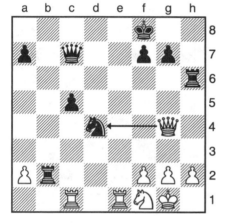

Handoko – Chon
Zonal tournament, Manila 2001

In the diagram, the three relevant units are the rook on c1, the queen on c7 and the intervening pawn on c5. In a pin, a friendly line-moving piece lies on the same line as two enemy pieces. Both enemy pieces are on the same side of the friendly piece. We call the nearer enemy piece (in this case the pawn) the **pinned piece** and the distant enemy piece (here the queen) the **rear piece**. If the pinned piece moves off the line of the pin, then the rear enemy piece can be captured. In this case, the c5-pawn is defending the d4-knight, but this protection is more apparent than real, because if Black actually plays ...cxd4, then

White will be able to play ♖xc7, winning Black's queen. White exploited this situation by playing **23 ♕xd4** (*see next diagram*), when Black immediately resigned.

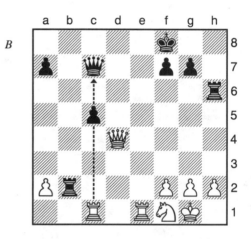

If Black ignores the capture then he stays a knight down, but 23...cxd4 24 ♖xc7 does not help him; the queens are exchanged, but his material deficit remains.

When the rear piece is not the king, the pin may or may not result in the immediate loss of material – it all depends on the values of the pieces involved. In the above case, White lost a queen, while Black lost a queen and a knight, so the net result was that White gained a knight. However, if Black's queen had been defended, so that he could have taken White's rook on c7 at the end, then the material balance would have shifted in Black's favour and so he would have avoided material loss. The more valuable the rear piece is, the more likely it is that the pin will lose material, but each case much be treated individually.

If the rear piece is the king, then the situation is different because the pinned piece cannot move off the pin-line at all, and so the material values are less important.

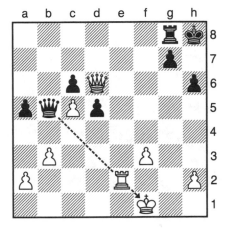

Rublevsky – Vaganian
Olympiad, Elista 1998

Here Black's queen is pinning the white rook against the white king. The rook has no legal moves, so Black can attack it with impunity. After **37...♖e8** White resigned since the rook is now attacked twice, and White is unable to defend it a second time.

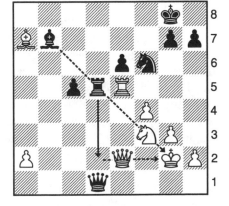

Donguines – Adianto
Asian Ch, Calcutta 2001

This position shows that it can be hard to see more complex tactics involving pins. It looks as though the d2-square is adequately defended, but Black realized that he can indeed play **34...♖d2!**. White resigned straight away because he loses his queen thanks to a double pin. The f3-knight is pinned by the b7-bishop, while the queen on e2 is pinned by Black's rook. How can one see such tactics in advance? In most cases there are clues which alert players can spot. Here the line-up of the b7-bishop and White's king is the key feature; looking at this reveals that any move by the d5-rook will totally paralyse White's knight, rendering it incapable of guarding any square. That leads naturally to the d2-square, and the lethal second pin.

If you are lucky then you may be able to win material with an immediate pin, but few opponents are so helpful as to lose material in one move. In most cases the pin has to be prepared; this will usually involve forcing moves such as captures and checks.

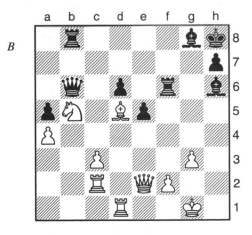

Topalov – Lautier
Tilburg 1998

The f2-pawn is pinned by Black's queen, but this observation leads to no immediate win. However, by means of a preliminary sacrifice Black can force White's queen to replace the pawn, providing a much more worthwhile target for a pin. The game continued **30...♖xf2!** **31 ♕xf2** (White must accept, or he faces catastrophic material loss) **31...♗e3** (now White's queen is pinned, and Black ends up winning a queen and pawn for a rook and a bishop) **32 ♔g2 ♗xf2 33 ♖xf2 ♕e3 34 ♘xd6** (Black has a decisive material advantage in any case, but he can win the game quickly with some further tactics) **34...♖b1! 0-1**. White resigned since he loses more material; for example, 35 ♖xb1 ♗xd5+ 36 ♔g1 ♕xg3+ 37 ♔f1 ♕d3+ winning the b1-rook, or 35 ♗f3 ♖xd1 36 ♗xd1 ♕d3 attacking pieces on d1 and d6.

Although most pins operate against enemy pieces, it is also possible to pin a piece against a threat, such as a potential mate.

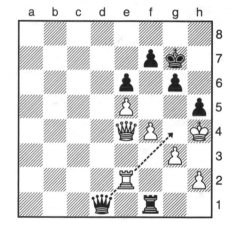

Tiviakov – Volokitin
Esbjerg 2002

In this position the white rook is pinned, even though there is no other white piece on the pin-line. If the rook moves, then Black has instant mate by ...♕g4#, so the rook is immobilized in much the same way as if it were pinned against the king. Black played **53...♖f2** (53...♖e1 is also good) and White resigned since the second attack on his rook leaves him facing loss of material.

A pin can tie up the opposing pieces so much that the attacker can afford to spend some time bringing further pressure to bear on the pinned piece.

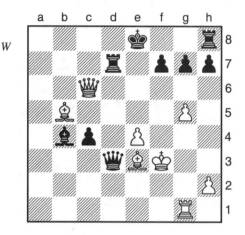

Shabalov – Istratescu
Olympiad, Elista 1998

White has sacrificed considerable material to reach this position, and is currently the exchange and a pawn down. Therefore it would not do simply to take twice on d7; although this would regain the exchange, White would then be a pawn down in the endgame. In order to end up ahead on material, White must aim to win the pinned d7-rook for nothing. Thus he must bring further pressure to bear on Black's position. Note that White's e3-bishop is itself pinned, so cannot play an active role. This pinned bishop also prevents White from playing 27 ♕c8+ ♔e7 28 ♕xh8, as then 28...♗d2 would win material for Black. The white piece which is currently playing little part in the action is the rook on g1. White must seek to activate this rook, but although the pin holds Black captive for the moment, he is threatening to escape his bonds by ...♔e7 (although Black can still legally castle, this would drop a whole rook on d7), releasing the rook for action. White played **27 ♗a4!** (27 ♖a1 is less effective due to 27...♔e7), threatening 28 ♖d1. Although this might seem a rather slow plan, there is nothing Black can do to avoid decisive material loss; for example, 27...♗e7 28 ♖d1 ♕xd1+ 29 ♗xd1 ♖xd1 30 ♕b7+, winning the b4-bishop. The game actually finished **27...f5 28 ♖d1** and Black resigned, because after 28...♕xe4+ 29 ♕xe4+ fxe4+ 30 ♔xe4 Black will lose a whole rook on d7, ending up a piece down. This example is typical in that the attacker is able to take his time stepping up the pressure on the pinned piece, but he has to bear in mind the possibility of the defender unpinning.

As with all the tactics described in this book, one must always analyse each position individually to make sure that the intended continuation really works. When you are thinking about your own tactical possibilities, it is easy to overlook tactics by the opponent.

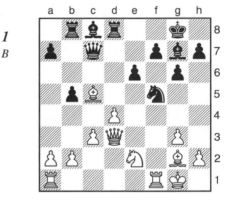

Medrano – Borda
Pan American Junior Ch, La Paz 2002

This position illustrates a familiar opening trap arising after the moves **1 d4 d5 2 c4 e6 3 ♘c3 ♘f6 4 ♗g5 ♘bd7 5 cxd5 exd5**. Black's f6-knight is pinned against his queen and it appears that White can win a pawn by playing **6 ♘xd5**. However, this runs into a surprising refutation: **6...♘xd5! 7 ♗xd8 ♗b4+**

8 ♕d2 ♗xd2+ 9 ♔xd2 ♔xd8 and Black wins a piece. The quoted game concluded **10 e4 ♘5f6 11 ♗d3 ♘b6 12 ♘f3 ♗e7 13 ♖he1 ♖d8 14 h3 c6 15 ♖ad1 ♔f8 16 ♔c1 ♗e6 17 ♗b1 ♖ac8 18 ♘h2 ♘h5 19 ♖f1 ♗c4 20 ♖fe1 ♘f4 21 g3 ♘e2+ 0-1**. It is worth knowing about this trap because it arises frequently in practice – my database contains no fewer than 132 examples of it.

Pin Exercises

Solutions start on page 121.

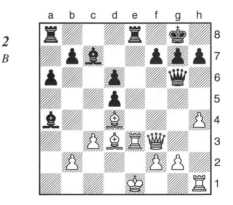

How did Black win material using a pin?

Black's queen is under attack. What should he play?

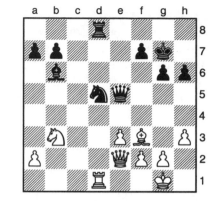

How did White set up a decisive pin?

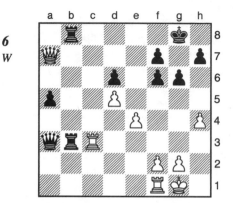

How can White win material?

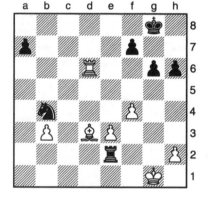

How should Black continue?

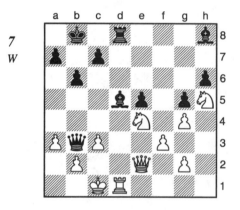

How did White gain material?

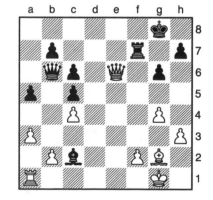

Which move caused Black to resign immediately?

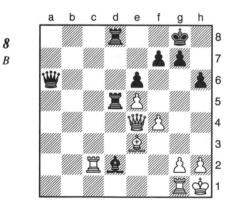

How did Black win material by means of a pin?

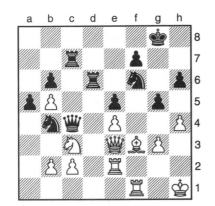

9
B

In this position Black won a vital pawn. How?

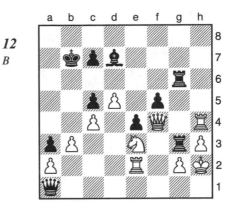

12
B

How did Black use a pin to bring the game to a rapid conclusion?

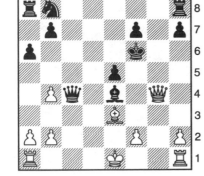

10
W

How did White win quickly?

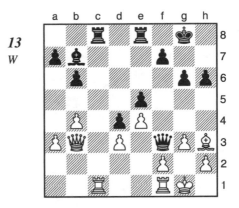

13
W

White played **23 ♗xc8**. Was this a good move?

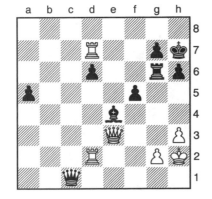

11
B

What is Black's quickest route to victory?

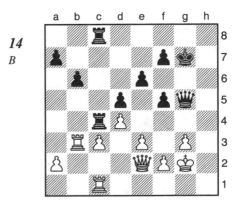

14
B

Can Black win a pawn using two pins?

15
W

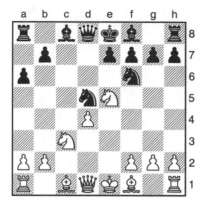

How did White win material?

18
W

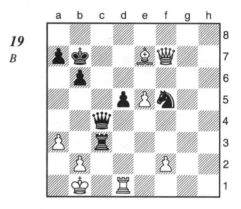

How did White step up the pressure and win material?

16
B

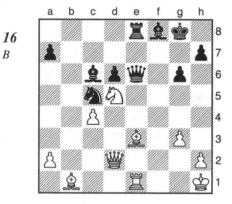

How did Black win material?

19
B

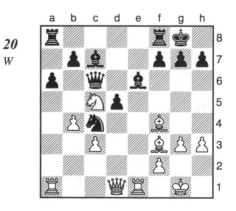

How did Black win material using a pin?

17
W

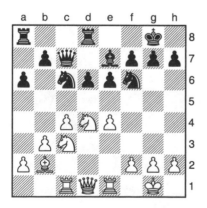

The position looks harmless enough, but White won material using a pin. How?

20
W

How did White set up and exploit a pin?

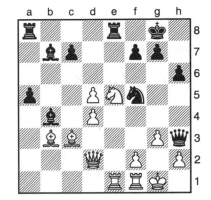

21
B

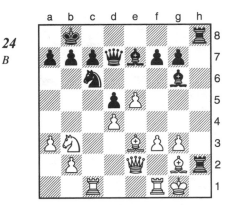

24
B

Two forcing moves finished White off. How?

How did Black win material?

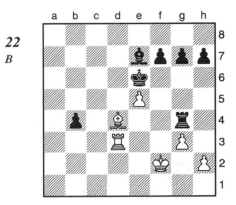

22
B

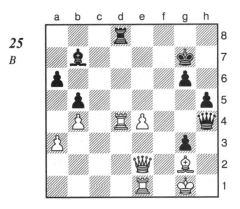

25
B

How did Black finish the game off quickly?

Does Black have anything better than the capture 35...♖xd4?

23
B

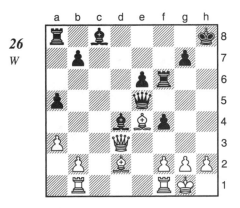

26
W

Find a decisive combination for Black.

How did White pin and win?

27
W

How did White win a vital pawn?

30
B

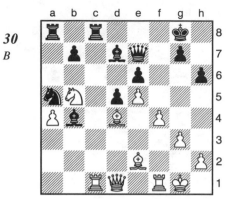

How did Black win material?

28
W

Can White take the pawn on a6?

31
W

Does **28 ♘xe6 fxe6 29 ♖e5** win material?

29
B

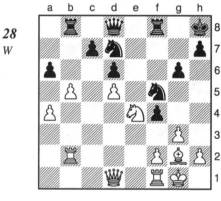

Black played the pinning combination **31...♕xg5 32 ♕xg5 gxh5**. Was this a good idea?

4 Skewer

The skewer is a tactical device closely related to the pin; indeed the geometrical arrangement is exactly the same. Here is an example:

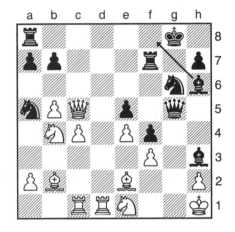

Cebalo – Ferčec
Croatian Ch, Pula 1998

Black spotted the line-up of White's queen and b4-knight and played **26...♗f8**, attacking the queen (*see next diagram*).

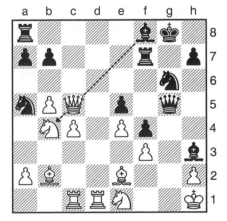

The queen had to move, but then Black could take the knight for free. After **27 ♕f2 ♗xb4** Black was a piece up and soon won.

The essence of a skewer is that a friendly line-moving piece lies on the same line as two enemy pieces, with both enemy pieces on the same side of the friendly piece. Thus far it is the same as a pin, but now comes the crucial difference. In a pin the nearer enemy piece is less valuable than the more distant enemy piece, while in a skewer it is the other way around. In the above example, the queen was more valuable than the knight. The queen, when attacked by the bishop, had to move, exposing the knight to capture. Skewers occur less often than pins, but still represent an important tactical device.

A particularly important case arises when the front (more valuable) piece is the king, since then the defender may have no choice but to move it.

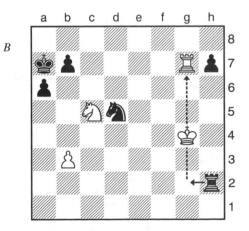

Svirin – Batsanin
Russian Team Ch, St Petersburg 1999

White has just played **43 ♘e4-c5?** and he now resigned without waiting for his opponent to play 43...♖g2+. Then White has to move his king, allowing Black to take the rook on g7 for nothing. Skewers which are also checks arise quite often in the endgame.

As with the other tactical motifs in this book, it may be necessary to prepare the skewer with a preliminary manoeuvre.

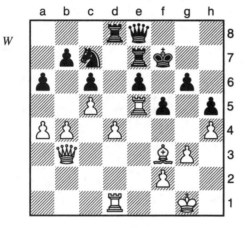

Berkes – Cao Sang
Budapest 2001

In this position White won material with the spectacular move **36 ♖xf5+!**, which exploits a variety of geometrical ideas. Firstly, Black cannot take this rook with his e6-pawn, because it is pinned by White's queen. Secondly, 36...gxf5 is met by 37 ♗xh5+, skewering Black's king and queen. The result would be that White would win a queen and two pawns for a rook and a bishop, a significant material gain. In view of this, Black replied **36...♔g7**, simply acquiescing to the loss of an important pawn. White wrapped the game up by **37 ♖g5 ♖f7 38 ♗xh5 ♖f6 39 ♗f3 ♕f7 40 ♗e4 ♖h8 41 ♕e3 ♘d5 42 ♗xd5 exd5 43 ♖e5 ♖f3 44 ♕e2 ♕f6 45 ♖e7+ ♔h6 46 ♕d2+ ♔h5 47 ♖e5+ ♔g4 48 ♖g5+ ♔h3 49 ♕e2 1-0**, with Black unable to avoid mate by ♕f1#.

Skewer Exercises

Solutions start on page 126.

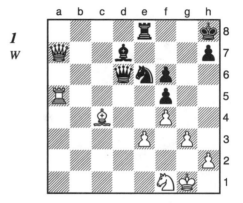

How did White win material?

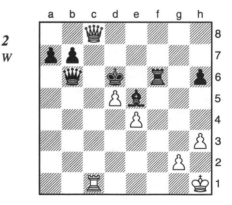

Currently White is a piece for a pawn down. How did he regain the piece and reach a winning position?

3
B

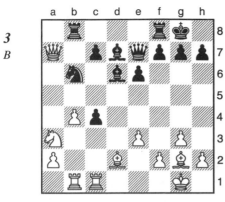

How can Black win material?

5
B

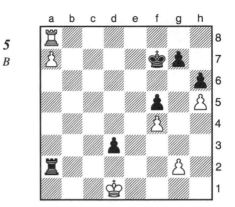

Black played **36...g6** here. Was this a good move?

4
B

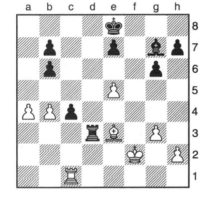

How did Black finish White off?

6
B

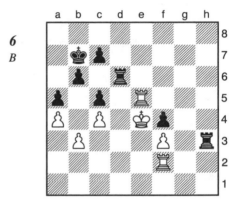

How did Black force a win in this apparently placid position?

5 Deflection

In the earlier chapters of this book, the tactics depended on the geometrical arrangement of the pieces on the board; for example, pins and skewers are based on the lining-up of the pieces involved. Not all tactics are of this type. In this chapter we meet for the first time tactics which depend on the **functions** of the pieces involved rather than the geometry of the chessboard.

A deflection arises when an enemy piece has an important duty. If it is forcibly pulled away from its current position, then it may no longer be able to fulfil its duty, and catastrophe ensues.

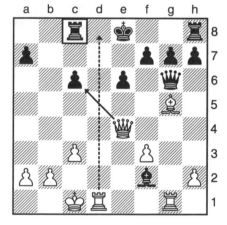

Marciano – Prié
French Ch, Narbonne 1997

In the diagram, Black's c8-rook has a vital responsibility – covering d8 so as to prevent White from mating by ♖d8#. If it is forced to abandon this duty then the game will end at once. It follows that the rook is unable to exercise any influence along the file, and therefore its defence of the c6-pawn is apparent

rather than real. White played **20 ♕xc6+**, placing Black in a dilemma. After 20...♖xc6, White can reply 21 ♖d8#, while the only other legal move, 20...♔f8, allows 21 ♕xc8#. Black therefore resigned.

The important duty which forms the basis for a deflection doesn't have to be defence against a mate threat, although this is a common motif. In the following example it is the defence of another piece.

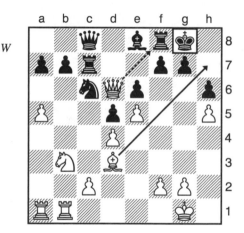

A. Horvath – Priehoda
Mitropa Cup, Leipzig 2002

Here Black's king has the duty of defending the rook on f8, which is under attack by White's queen. Unlike a mating threat, the duty of defending a piece **can** be abandoned, albeit at the cost of the piece in question. Whether the deflection is worthwhile depends on the relative value of the pieces in question; if the attacker wins a more valuable piece by sacrificing a less valuable one, then the tactic is worthwhile. White continued **23 ♗h7+**

♔xh7 24 ♕xf8. By giving up a bishop, he deflected Black's king away from the defence of the rook and thereby won the exchange, securing a winning position. When you have won material, it is important not to relax and assume that the game will win itself. The rest of this game is a perfect example of how **not** to exploit a material advantage. White carelessly became embroiled in unnecessary complications, miscalculated some tactics and eventually even lost: **24...b6 25 axb6 axb6 26 ♖a3 ♘b8 27 ♖a8 ♖xc2 28 ♘c5 ♕d8 29 ♕d6?** (29 g3! would have snuffed out Black's counterplay and won easily) **29...♕h4 30 ♘d3?** (30 ♖f1 was still winning) **30...♘c6 31 ♖xe8 ♘xd4 32 ♖e1 ♘f3+ 33 gxf3 ♕g5+ 34 ♔f1 ♕xh5 35 ♔g2 ♕g6+ 36 ♔f1?** (36 ♔h2 ♕xd3 37 ♖g1 would still have drawn) **36...♕xd3+ 37 ♔g2 ♕d2 38 ♖f1 ♕g5+ 39 ♔h2 ♖c4 40 ♕e7 ♖h4#.**

It is quite common for deflections to play a major role in attacks on the king.

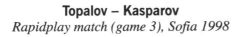

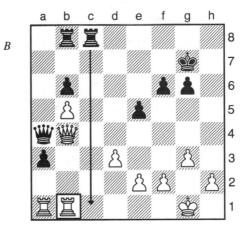

Bui Vinh – Frey
Olympiad, Bled 2002

while 48 ♔h2 is also mate after 48...♖h1# or 48...♕h1#. This deflection is harder to see than those in the examples given above because the white king's important duty isn't obvious in the diagram – ...♕h1+ is hardly a move one would consider while the white king is still guarding h1. Chess cannot be played successfully by rote and a certain degree of imagination is necessary to spot many ideas.

One type of deflection occurs time and time again in practice and regularly catches out players of all levels, up to and including grandmasters. Here is a recent example.

Topalov – Kasparov
Rapidplay match (game 3), Sofia 1998

Here Black is a piece down, and in addition his d4-knight is caught in a pin. It might seem hopeless, but Black actually won with the aid of a deflection: **47...♖xf1+**. White resigned as 48 ♔xf1 is met by 48...♕h1#,

White's b1-rook has the important duty of defending the queen. If this rook could be deflected away, then White would lose his queen. **32...♖c1+** does the trick. After 33 ♖xc1 ♕xb4 Black has won a queen for a rook, while after 33 ♔g2 Black wins a rook with the characteristic continuation 33...♕xb4 34 ♖xb4 ♖xa1, exploiting a kind of pin along the first rank. White therefore resigned. The typical features of this tactic are a rook on the first rank defending a queen, and an enemy rook which can land on the first rank with check. It is amazing how often this trick occurs in practice; for some reason it is incredibly easy to overlook.

In all the examples given so far, the deflecting move has been a check. Since checks are such forcing moves, it is not surprising that they occur frequently in this type of tactic. However, non-checking deflections are also quite common.

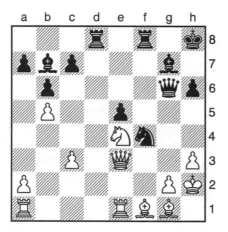

Cifuentes – Reinderman
Dutch Ch, Rotterdam 1999

White's f1-bishop has the 'important duty' of preventing ...♕xg2#, so it is not genuinely covering the d3-square. Black exploited this by **29...♖d3!**, attacking White's queen. The queen also has a duty, that of guarding the knight on e4. A quick check shows that the queen has no move which still defends the e4-knight, and so White must lose material. The game continued **30 ♕xd3** (this looks like a reasonable chance, giving up the queen for a rook and a knight, but it turns out that White faces further material loss) **30...♘xd3 31 ♗xd3 ♖d8** and White resigned. If he defends the bishop by 32 ♖ad1, then 32...♖xd3 33 ♖xd3 ♗xe4 gives Black queen and bishop for two rooks, while after 32 ♗b1 (32 ♗c2 ♖d2 is the same) 32...♖d2! White has no reasonable way to defend against the mate threat on g2 (note that the e4-knight is pinned, so

that 33 ♘xd2 is met by 33...♕xg2#). In all cases White faces catastrophic material loss.

As with all the tactical elements covered in this book, deflections can occur with varying degrees of complexity. The next example is a little more involved.

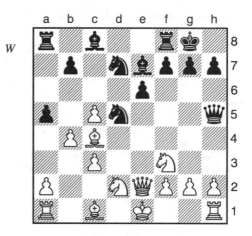

Beshukov – Jenetl
Krasnodar 1999

Black's queen has the 'important duty' of defending the knight on d5. At first sight the queen is not needed because the d5-knight is defended by the e6-pawn, but this pawn is pinned by the white queen. In other words, if the queen were not defending d5 then White could win a piece by playing ♗xd5, meeting ...exd5 by ♕xe7. This leads us to the winning move **12 g4!**, after which the queen cannot retain its defence of d5. White wins a piece and the game concluded **12...♕xg4 13 ♗xd5 exd5 14 ♕xe7 ♘f6 15 ♖g1 ♕f4 16 ♕d6 ♕h6 17 ♘e4** and Black resigned since White's threats of 18 ♗xh6 and 18 ♘xf6+ win further material.

Sometimes a preliminary action is necessary before the actual deflection takes place. A deflection is not apparent in the following diagram, but White set one up with a preliminary sacrifice: **25 ♖xd5! exd5** (Black can

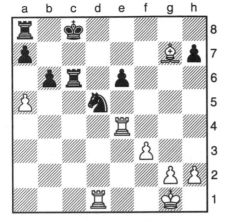

P. Cramling – Barkhagen
Hasselbacken 2001

insert some checks, but 25...♖c1+ 26 ♔f2 ♖c2+ 27 ♔g3 doesn't change the situation) **26 ♖e8+ ♔b7** (the only square for the king; otherwise White can take the a8-rook immediately) **27 a6+!** (here is the deflection; Black's king must abandon the important duty of defending the rook) **27...♔xa6 28 ♖xa8** (White has won a piece for a pawn; Black soon gave up) **28...♖c7 29 ♗e5 ♖d7 30 ♔f2 1-0**.

In the following example, the deflection is combined with other tactical elements.

Kogan – Samaritani
Bled 1998

This position looks rather confusing, with both sides having advanced pawns, but White won the game with a neat combination: **29 ♖h8+!** (this deflection allows White to take on f7 without the king recapturing) **29...♔xh8 30 gxf7** (suddenly White has two deadly threats, 31 ♖h1# and 31 fxe8♛+; there is no defence against both) **30...bxa2++ 31 ♔xa2 1-0**. Black resigned because after 31...♖b2+ 32 ♔a1 he runs out of checks and cannot meet White's threats. In this case the deflection was combined with pawn promotion and with the creation of mating threats.

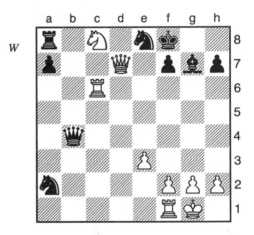

Dreev – Svidler
European Clubs Cup, Kallithea 2002

This example is even more complex. Black has a bishop and knight for a rook and a pawn, so material is roughly equal. A more important factor is the activity of several white pieces, but for the moment there is no direct way to break through. A queen check on e7 would be decisive, but Black's queen covers this square. However, Dreev noticed that this is an important duty for the black queen, and he went on to look for a way the queen could be deflected away from this duty. The game continued with the sacrifice **26 ♖c4!**, trying to force the queen to quit the a3-f8 diagonal. If Black plays 26...♛a3, then

27 ♖e4 wins (the e8-knight is attacked, and after 27...♘f6 White mates by 28 ♕d8+), so Black must accept the sacrifice. The forced continuation is 26...♕xc4 27 ♕e7+ ♔g8 28 ♕xe8+ ♗f8 29 ♘e7+ ♔g7 30 ♘f5+! (better than 30 ♕xa8 ♗xe7 31 ♕xa7, which only leaves White slightly ahead on material) 30...♔f6 31 ♕xa8 ♔xf5 32 ♕xf8 and White is the exchange and a pawn up, a decisive material advantage. Black saw all this and therefore resigned. Although this combination was quite deep, most of it was forced and the really difficult part was having the idea for the deflection in the first place. Then it was a matter of calculating whether the material White gains by checking on e7 outweighs the initial rook sacrifice.

We end with a form of deflection which is subtly different from the examples we have seen so far.

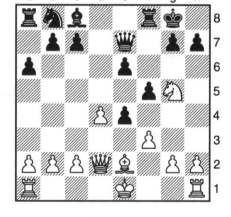

Bhuiyan – Liogky
Sautron 2001

White's queen has the important task of defending the outlying knight on g5, but there is no way to deflect the queen **away** from this duty. Instead Black wins a piece by drawing the queen **onto** an especially unfavourable square. The game continued **11...e3** and White resigned as after 12 ♕xe3 f4 (e3 is

a bad square for the queen as this move, cutting the queen's guard of g5, comes with gain of tempo) 13 ♕e5 ♖f5 he ends up a piece down.

The distinction between this idea, which is often called a 'decoy', and that of deflection may at first seem obscure, as in both cases a forcing move compels an opposing piece to take an unfavourable action. The difference is that in a deflection it is the departure of the enemy piece which is unfavourable, while in a decoy it is the arrival of the enemy piece on a particularly bad square which is unfavourable. The terminology for these different motifs is not wholly standard; the words 'decoy', 'diversion' and 'deflection' are used to mean different things by different writers. In this book our focus is on winning games, and not on the nuances of chess terminology; therefore for simplicity we will use the word 'deflection' for all such ideas.

Deflection Exercises

Solutions start on page 127.

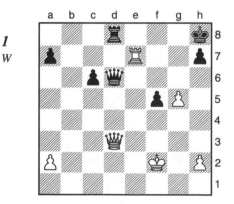

White is a pawn down. What should he play?

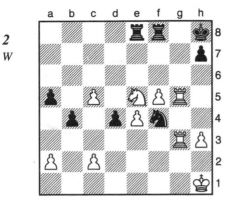

2
W

What is the simplest win for White?

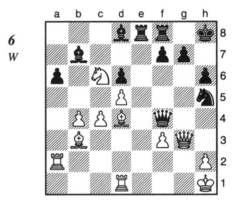

5
W

Black resigned after White's next move. What was it?

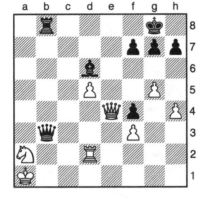

3
B

How did Black force a quick mate?

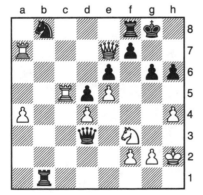

6
W

How did White win material?

4
W

What is White's quickest way of pushing his attack home?

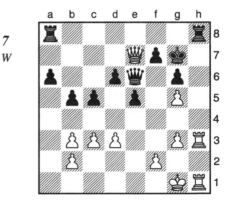

7
W

How did White win a rook with a deflection?

8
W

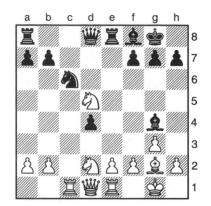

White played **16 h3** in this game between two top grandmasters. Was this a good move?

11
B

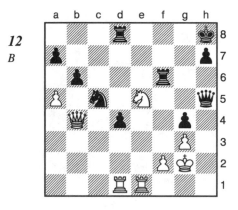

Deflections can also occur in the endgame. How did Black win here?

9
B

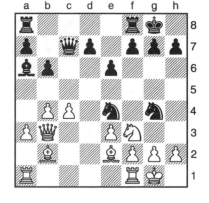

A deflection secured Black a decisive material advantage. How?

12
B

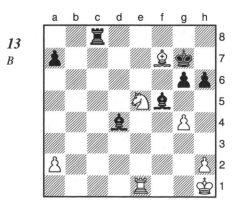

How did Black use a deflection to force a quick mate?

10
W

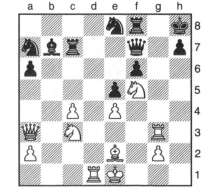

How does White win most easily?

13
B

How did Black end the game with a single deadly blow?

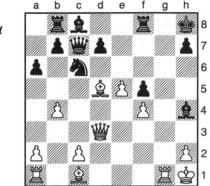

14
W

White has sacrificed a piece for a strong initiative. How did he press his attack home?

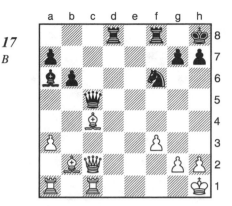

17
B

Black played **25...♖c8** and the game ended in a draw. Did he have a better move?

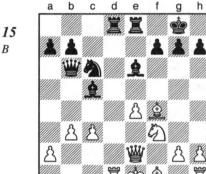

15
B

How did Black force material gain?

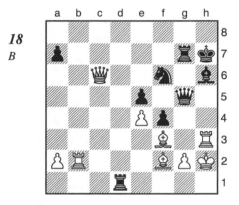

18
B

How did Black force an instant win?

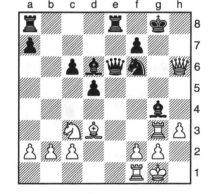

16
W

White has sacrificed a piece. How did he win with a deflection?

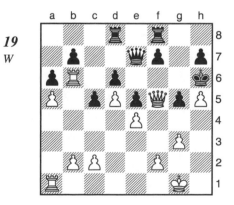

19
W

White used a deflection to start a decisive attack on Black's king. How?

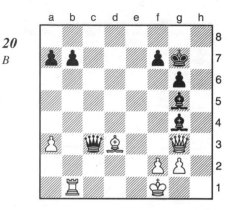

20
B

A deflection forced immediate resignation.
How?

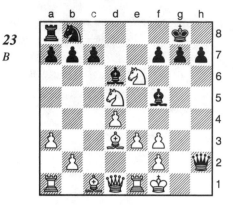

23
B

How did Black force a quick mate?

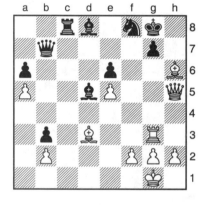

21
W

White has sacrificed a piece. How did he
force his attack home?

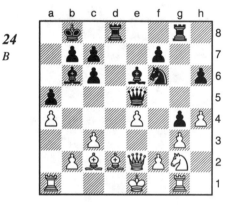

24
B

How did Black win using two consecutive
deflections?

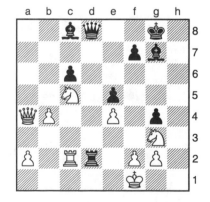

22
B

How did Black win with a double deflection?

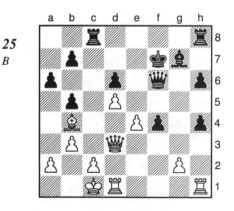

25
B

How did Black win with a preliminary sacrifice followed by a deflection?

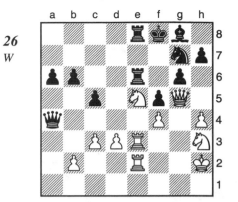

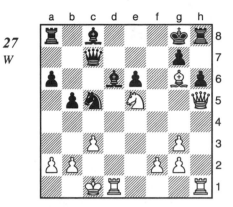

How did White break Black's resistance?

A tough one to end with. How did White win with two deflections?

6 Trapped Piece

Piece mobility is extremely important in chess; a piece with little mobility is less valuable than one which has a wide-ranging influence on the game. An extreme case is a piece which has no safe square at all. If such a piece is attacked it may well be lost.

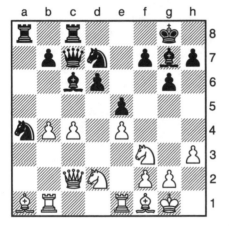

Slobodian – Bangiev
German Ch, Dudweiler 1996

This position shows the idea. Black's last move was the unfortunate **19...♘f6-d7?**. This took away the last remaining safe squares for the c6-bishop, namely d7 and e8. White continued **20 b5** and the poor bishop had nowhere to go. Faced with the loss of his bishop for a mere pawn, Black immediately resigned.

In the above case the piece was trapped in friendly territory. If a piece goes on an adventurous but unwise journey into the enemy half of the board, the chances of it being trapped increase.

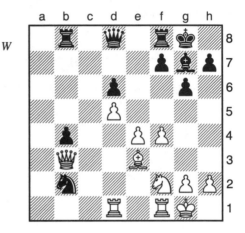

Dreev – Saldano
European Clubs Cup, Kallithea 2002

Black's knight has embarked on a lonely journey to b2. Admittedly, it is defended by the g7-bishop, but it lacks any support from Black's other pieces. If White can cut off the bishop's defence, then the knight will be trapped. White achieved this aim by moving his attacked rook to the long diagonal: **25 ♖d4!**. Of course Black can reply 25...♗xd4, but after 26 ♗xd4 the knight will fall next move, and White will have won a bishop and a knight for a rook. Moreover, Black's dark squares, especially on the kingside, would be horribly weak so this position would be lost for Black. Therefore Black tried to confuse the issue with **25...♕a5** but White kept a clear head and won convincingly: **26 ♕xb2 b3 27 e5! ♖fe8 28 ♖d2 dxe5 29 fxe5 ♖b5 30 ♘e4 ♖xd5 31 ♕xb3 1-0**. Black is already a piece down and faces further material loss because the d5-rook is pinned against a deadly queen check on f7.

This example reinforces the point that pieces which embark on aggressive operations can rarely succeed without support from the rest of the army; solo actions are more likely to end in disaster than triumph. This applies particularly to the queen. Despite its great mobility, a queen can easily be trapped if it ventures alone into enemy territory. Rooks, knights and bishops are all worth less than the queen, and by acting in concert they can surround and capture a reckless queen.

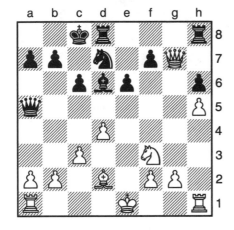

de Firmian – A. Ivanov
USA Ch, Seattle 2000

White has just grabbed the g-pawn by **17 ♕g4xg7?**, calculating that if Black starts chasing the queen with his rooks then White will grab the f7-pawn, and eventually return to d3 via g6 or h7. However, Black made use of an important principle which often helps when trying to trap a piece: rather than aimlessly attacking the piece again and again, eventually chasing it back to safety, it is often better to cut off the piece's retreat route, and then play to trap it. After **17...♕f5!**, White suddenly found himself in serious trouble. The threat is 18...♖dg8 and the free tempo is not of much help as the white queen has no safe squares. The game continued **18 ♘h4** (18 d5 frees the d4-square for the queen, but after 18...♗e5 19 ♘xe5 ♘xe5 20 ♕g3 ♖hg8

White's position collapses; for example, 21 ♕h3 ♘d3+ or 21 ♕e3 ♖xg2) **18...♕e4+ 19 ♔d1 ♖h7** (the queen is trapped in any case) **20 f3** and now 20...♕d3! 21 ♕g4 ♘f6 22 ♕h3 ♗f4 would have won at once. Black played instead **20...♕xh4 21 ♖xh4 ♖xg7** with an extra piece, which also proved sufficient for eventual victory.

Of course, every piece of advice has its exceptions and there are some cases in which a queen can grab an enemy pawn and then return safely. However, all such cases have to be calculated very carefully to make sure that the queen can make it back. Even experienced grandmasters sometimes get it wrong, as in the previous diagram.

Many pieces are trapped because of the element of surprise. If a piece has several squares available, the player may simply not take into account the possibility of the piece getting trapped; if it doesn't 'look' as if the piece can be trapped, there is no sense of danger.

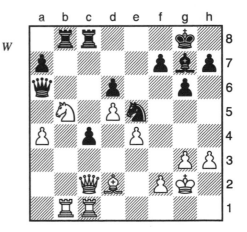

Gretarsson – Stefansson
Icelandic Ch, Seltjarnarnes 2002

Here it appears unlikely that White will even manage to attack Black's queen; in addition, the queen seems able to move to b6 if necessary. However, **24 ♘c7!** proved that appearances can be deceptive. The b1-rook's line of attack along the b-file is uncovered, and this takes away the last squares from the queen. Moreover, it turns out that although c7 was apparently guarded by the c8-rook, White can in fact move his knight there with impunity as 24...♖xc7 is met by 25 ♖xb8+ winning the exchange. The upshot is that Black faces a fatal loss of material; the finish was **24...♖xb1 25 ♘xa6 ♖xc1 26 ♗xc1 ♘d3 27 ♗d2 ♗d4 28 ♘b4 1-0**.

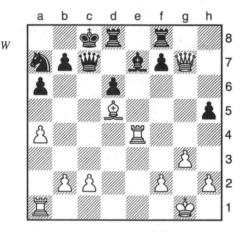

de la Riva – Plaskett
Zonal tournament, Mondariz 2000

In this case the black bishop's lack of mobility allows White to win material by combining several tactical ideas. He played **21 ♖ae1**, attacking the bishop. The bishop has no safe square, so Black's only hope of saving it is to defend it. However, 21...♘c6 fails to 22 ♗xc6, removing the bishop's guard. Alternatively, after 21...♖fe8 22 ♕xf7 White wins material thanks to the deadly pin along the e-file. Finally, Black can try defending the bishop with the d8-rook, as in the game. The conclusion was **21...♖de8** (21...♖d7 loses the same way) **22 ♖xe7** and Black resigned, since 22...♖xe7 23 ♕xf8+ is catastrophic for him. This last variation shows a deflection motif.

Trapped Piece Exercises

Solutions start on page 131.

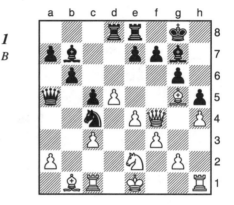

How did Black finish the game at a stroke?

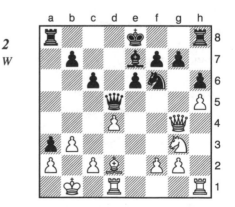

White played **20 ♕xg7**. Can he get away with this?

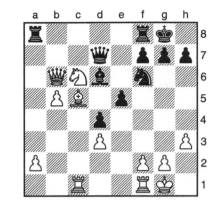

3
B

Which piece did Black manage to trap?

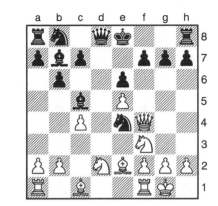

6
B

How did Black force a material gain?

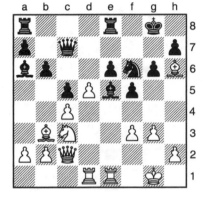

4
W

How can White set up a winning piece trap?

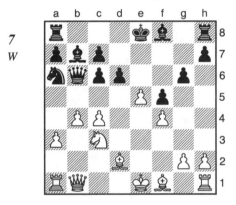

7
W

At the moment Black's queen can flee to d4. How did White cut off this escape-route?

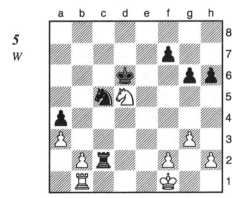

5
W

How did White force a quick win?

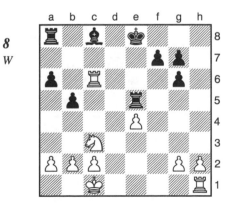

8
W

White has just seized an enemy pawn by **18 罝d6xc6**. Was this a good idea?

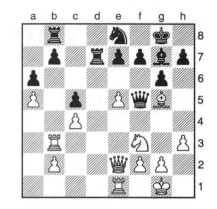

9
W

How did White win the game by trapping a black piece?

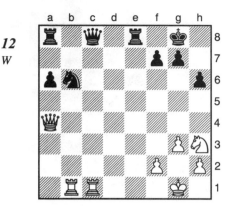

12
W

Black has just played **...♘d7xb6** hoping to win a pawn. What was the flaw in his idea?

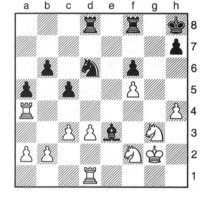

10
W

How did White trap a piece and win the game?

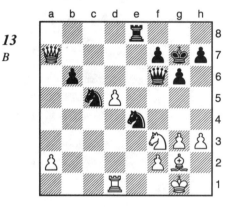

13
B

How did Black win material?

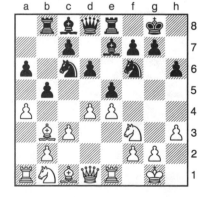

11
W

This position looks harmless, but White found a way to win material. How?

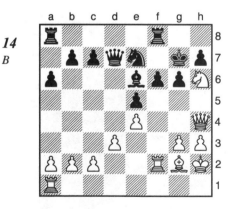

14
B

Two moves were enough to convince White to resign. What were they?

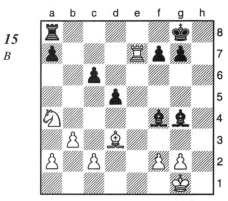

Is White's rook an asset or a liability?

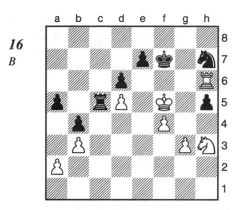

How did Black win material with a sequence of forcing moves?

7 Removing the Guard

This idea is best explained by means of an example.

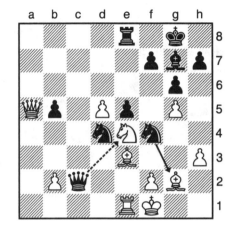

Socko – Nakamura
Bermuda 2002

Here White's g2-bishop has the function of defending the knight on e4. If the bishop is eliminated by an exchange, the knight will be undefended. Black therefore continued **27...♘xg2**, so that if White plays 28 ♔xg2, then 28...♕xe4+ wins a piece. White tried **28 ♗xd4**, but after **28...♘xe1 29 ♕xe1 ♕c4+** he resigned since 30...♕xd4 will leave him a rook down.

The basic situation is that one piece is defending a second one; when the first is eliminated by capture, the second can be taken for nothing. We shall call this **removing the guard**. However, there is no completely standard definition of this term in chess literature. In this book we extend the term to cover cases in which the first piece's vital duty may be something other than defending a second

piece. In the following position the vital duty is defending against a mate threat.

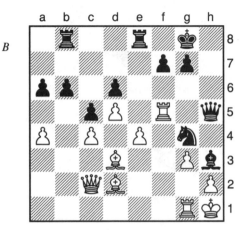

Chabanon – Bauer
French Ch, Narbonne 1997

White's f5-rook has the vital duty of preventing ...♘f2#. Black exploited this to play **32...♕xf5**, winning a rook for nothing. White resigned immediately.

Removing the guard is really a very general concept, since pieces take on and give up various duties all the time. However, we only apply the term when the removal of a piece has a specific short-term consequence, such as loss of material or mate. There are three common ways in which a piece can be compelled to give up an important duty. The first is deflection (see Chapter 5), when the piece is forcibly dragged away by a violent action elsewhere. The second is capture, as in the two examples above. The third is by a direct attack on the piece concerned, as in the following position. We also use the term removing the guard to cover this type of action.

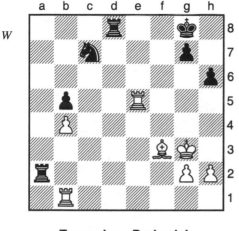

Tsesarsky – Berkovich
Israeli Team Ch 1997

Here the black knight has the duty of defending d5 so as to prevent the fork ♗d5+. White can attack this knight with one of his rooks, trying to force it to move. 34 ♖c5 is inferior as Black replies 34...♖a7, defending the knight and removing the rook from the vulnerable a2-square. The correct choice is **34 ♖c1!**, as played in the game. Black replied **34...♘a6**, just allowing the fork; after **35 ♗d5+ ♖xd5 36 ♖xd5 ♘xb4 37 ♖xb5** White was a clear exchange ahead and won using the extra material. Why did Black not defend the knight with one his rooks? After 34...♖d7 (34...♖c8 is even worse as 35 ♗d5+ wins a whole rook) White eliminates the knight by capture, as in the first two positions: 35 ♖xc7 ♖xc7 36 ♗d5+ and 37 ♗xa2, with an extra piece for White. The final possibility for Black is 34...♖a7, but after 35 ♖e7 the knight is pinned and Black can only avoid losing it immediately by 35...♖c8. Then there is a comical situation in which Black's entire army is paralysed by the need to defend the doubly pinned knight. The simplest win is by marching White's king up the board; for example, 36 ♖c6 (not 36 ♗g4?, when Black

unexpectedly unpins the knight by 36...♘e8!) 36...♔f8 37 ♖d7 ♔g8 38 ♔h4 ♔h8 39 ♔h5 ♔g8 40 ♔g6 and Black's position collapses.

Removing the Guard Exercises

Solutions start on page 134.

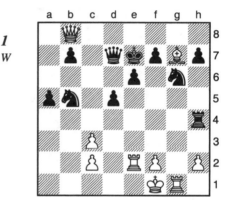

How did White win quickly by removing the guard?

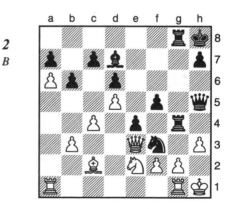

How did Black press home his kingside attack?

3
B

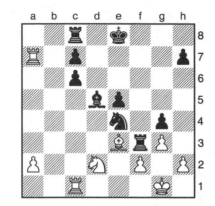

How did Black win material?

6
B

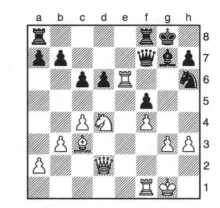

How can Black win material by removing the guard?

4
B

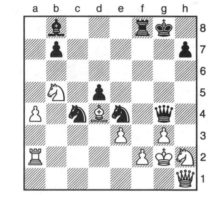

Black's queen is attacked. What is the best move?

7
B

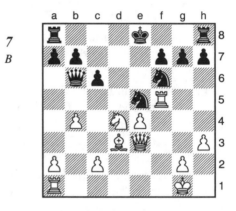

How did Black win an important pawn?

5
W

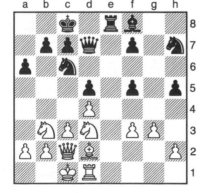

How did White force immediate resignation?

8
W

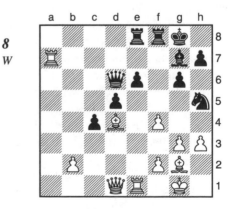

How did White force a decisive material gain?

8 Opening and Closing Lines

Many combinations are based on the opening of lines to allow friendly pieces access to squares which were formerly out of reach. When discussing such a general topic, there will of course be an overlap with some of the ideas discussed in earlier chapters (particularly deflection – see Chapter 5). However, this in itself is not an important point. Chess tactics do not necessarily fit into neat pigeon-holes with clear-cut labels on them. Even quite simple combinations may employ several different tactical motifs, while others sit uneasily on the boundary between one category and another. The important point is not whether one labels a particular combination 'line-opening' or 'deflection' – rather it is that knowing the combination can help win games. It is important not to adopt a blinkered approach to tactics, looking only for combinations based on knight forks or other familiar concepts; an open-minded attitude is far more likely to succeed. As we progress through the book we will encounter more complex combinations involving an amalgam of different ideas – indeed Chapter 13 is devoted to precisely this topic.

The following diagram shows a typical line-opening combination.

White won material with the neat continuation **16 ♘xd5!** (opening the c-file for the rook to reach c7) **16...cxd5 17 ♖c7**. This attacks the b7-bishop, and if Black should defend it by 17...♖ab8, then White continues 18 ♖xb7 ♖xb7 19 ♕xd5+ (fork) and 20 ♕xb7, ending up two pawns ahead. Since 17...♗a6 18 ♕xd5+ and 17...♘ec5 18 ♗xc5 cost Black at least a piece, it follows that Black has nothing better than to leave the attacked bishop

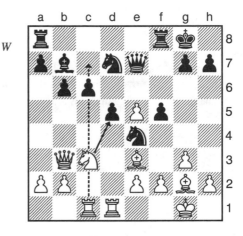

B. Kelly – R. Burnett
Budapest 2003

to its fate. The game continued **17...♕xe5 18 ♖xd7** and although material is now equal, Black's position is hopeless (*see diagram below*).

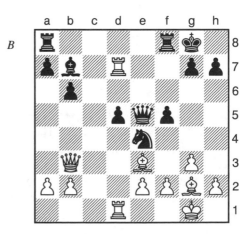

Black's b7-bishop is still under attack, and in addition White threatens 19 ♗d4 followed by 20 ♖xg7+. All this devastation is caused by the active position of White's rook on the seventh rank, which itself is the result of White's line-opening combination. The end was **18...♖f7 19 ♖xb7** and Black resigned, since 19...♖xb7 20 ♖xd5 (threatening both 21 ♖xe5+ and 21 ♖d8#) 20...♕e6 21 ♖d8+ picks up Black's queen.

This combination clearly involved several elements. Here the line-opening aspect has been emphasized, but the **deflection** of the c6-pawn is clearly important, as is the **fork** on d5 arising after 17...♖ab8 18 ♖xb7.

If the line which is to be opened points to the enemy king, then the line-opening can form part of a mating combination.

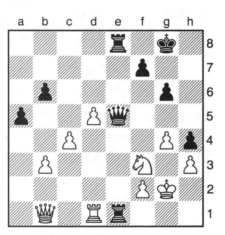

Moroz – Lerner
Vladikavkaz 2000

White resigned after **47...♕g3+!** since it's mate next move (48 fxg3 ♖8e2#). The sole purpose of the queen sacrifice was to open the second rank so that the e8-rook could deliver the final blow. Although this combination was only two moves deep, the grandmaster playing White evidently overlooked it (his last move was 47 ♘d4-f3?). It may seem surprising that a grandmaster could overlook a two-move-deep combination and the explanation is undoubtedly that Black's queen

sacrifice was rather unusual and not based on the standard patterns one normally finds in textbooks. This again emphasizes the point that although study of familiar patterns will undoubtedly improve one's playing strength, it is important not to lose the ability to think independently.

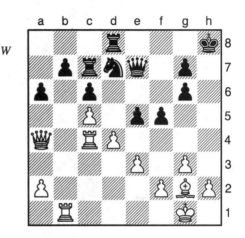

Stefansson – A. Gunnarsson
Icelandic Ch, Seltjarnarnes 2002

White played **26 d5!**, opening the fourth rank from c4 to h4. The normal response to White's pawn advance would be 26...cxd5, but thanks to the newly-opened line White can then win by 27 ♖h4+ ♚g8 28 ♗xd5+ and Black loses his queen or is mated after 28...♚f8 29 ♖h8#. Allowing White to play d6 is also horrible; for example, after 26...♕f7 27 d6 ♖cc8 28 ♖xb7 White wins a pawn (with more to come), has a powerful protected passed pawn and has caught Black in a pin along the seventh rank. Therefore Black went for his only other option, **26...♘xc5**, grabbing the pawn apparently left undefended by White's last move. However, **27 ♖xc5!** proved decisive, since after 27...♕xc5 White can make use of the whole width of the fourth rank with 28 ♕h4+ (fork) 28...♚g8 29 ♕xd8+, winning both black rooks. The game actually finished **27...e4 28 ♕a5 ♖xd5**

29 ℤxd5 cxd5 30 ♕xd5 ♔h7 31 a4 1-0. Here again the success of White's idea was based on a combination of ideas.

Just as it is often desirable to open a line for one's own pieces, closing a line for an enemy piece can prove equally effective.

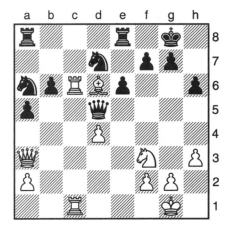

Strehlow – Biebinger
German Seniors Team Ch 2001

In this position White's pieces appear actively placed, but it turns out that the c6-rook is exposed. Black played **24...♘ac5!**, dropping his knight on apparently the best-defended square on the board. However, this move had the effect of closing the line c1-c6 and thereby cutting off the advanced rook's support. The game continued **25 ℤ6xc5** (25 ℤc7 ♕xd6 and 25 ♘e5 ♘xe5 only make matters worse) **25...bxc5 26 dxc5 ℤec8** (Black has secured a decisive material advantage and the rest is straightforward) **27 ♕a4 ♘xc5 28 ♗xc5 ℤxc5 29 ℤd1 ♕c4 30 ♕d7 ♕xa2 31 ℤd4 ♕b1+ 32 ♔h2 ♕b8+ 33 g3 ℤf5 34 ♔g2 0-1.**

Line-closing combinations commonly arise in two particular situations: pawn promotion and mating attacks. We give an example of the first case and you will see an example of the second in the exercises.

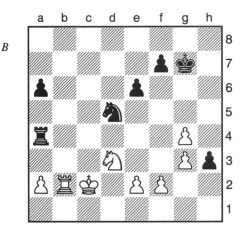

Averbakh – Korchnoi
Erevan 1965

At the moment, 38...h2 is ineffective because White can cover the queening square by 39 ℤb1. Therefore Black played a preliminary manoeuvre designed to close the defensive line b1-h1: **38...ℤc4+** and White resigned, since 39 ♔d2 is met by the sacrifice 39...ℤc1!. The diagram below shows the situation.

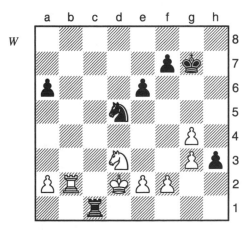

However White takes the rook, the first rank is blocked and the h-pawn runs through; for example, 40 ♘xc1 h2 or 40 ♔xc1 h2, followed by ...h1♕, and Black has a winning material advantage.

Opening and Closing Lines Exercises

Solutions start on page 135.

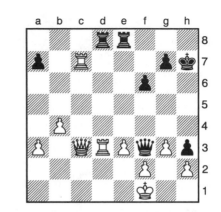

How did Black force mate?

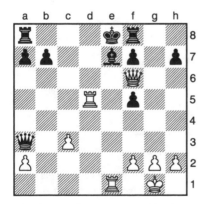

Which deadly blow did White strike here?

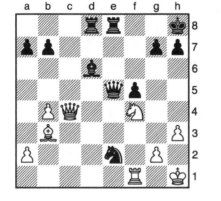

A confusing-looking position, but Black found a lethal move. What was it?

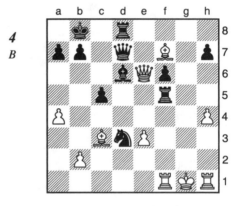

How did White press home his attack?

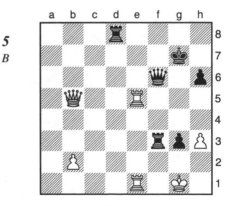

Here Black found a knock-out move. What was it?

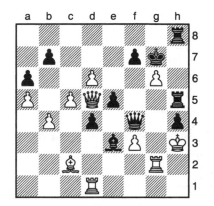

Both sides are attacking furiously, but how did Black strike first?

9 Back-Rank Mate

It quite often happens that the castled king is hemmed in by three friendly pawns on the second rank. This makes it vulnerable to a mate delivered by an enemy queen or rook arriving on the first rank. Such a mate is called a **back-rank mate**. Two conditions must be satisfied for such a mate to occur; first of all, the defender's resistance on the back rank must be inadequate, and secondly an enemy queen or rook must be able to penetrate to the back rank. Here is a simple example.

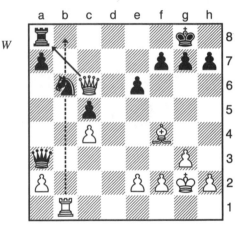

Kravtsov – Malinin
Russia Cup, Novgorod 1997

Black's king is blocked in by the three unmoved pawns in front of it, so there is a potential back-rank mate. However, Black still has a rook covering the back rank and this rook, for example, prevents mate by ♕e8#. In order to deliver a back-rank mate the resistance of this rook must be overcome; White achieved this by **20 ♕xa8+!**. Black resigned, since after 20...♘xa8 White plays 21 ♖b8#.

In this example White's queen sacrifice set up both conditions simultaneously; the rook was eliminated by capture and at the same time the b-file was opened to allow White's rook to deliver the mate.

Back-rank mates are unusual in the early middlegame, when there are usually two defensive rooks on the back rank. However, later on the rooks may leave the back rank or be exchanged off, and then the danger of a back-rank mate increases. Sometimes players spend a tempo playing g3 or h3 (...g6 or ...h6 for Black) specifically to create an escape-square and reduce the danger of a back-rank mate. However, such moves must be carefully judged since they can create weaknesses around the king; there is no general rule and each position must be treated individually.

The next example shows another typical back-rank idea.

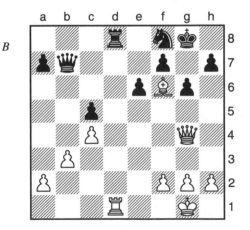

Xie Jun – Seirawan
'Queens vs Kings', Jinan 2002

White's king is vulnerable to a potential back-rank mate, and indeed if White's queen were not defending the d1-rook, then immediate mate by ...♖xd1# would be possible. This naturally raises the question as to whether White's queen can be compelled to give up the duty of guarding d1. Earlier in the book, we covered the three main ways in which a piece can be compelled to abandon a duty: capture, direct attack and deflection. Capture is not possible here, and the direct attack by 24...h5 achieves nothing after 25 ♕e2. That leaves deflection and leads us to the winning move **24...♕e4!**. White's queen is attacked, so he has no time to take on d8, but 25 ♕xe4 allows mate in two by 25...♖xd1+. Moreover, White's queen has no square available which retains control of d1, so, faced by catastrophic material loss, White resigned.

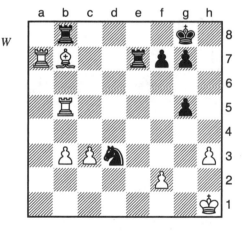

Topalov – Morozevich
Cannes 2002

White is a pawn up, but his bishop is doubly pinned and his f2-pawn is attacked. At first sight there cannot be a bank-rank mate in this position, because Black's h-pawn has moved, giving the king a flight-square. However, it is important to recognize that back-rank mates can still occur even when one (or more) of the pawns in front of the king has

moved, since the escape-square(s) can be covered by enemy pieces. Indeed, practice shows that back-rank mates of this type are frequently overlooked. The reason is likely to be psychological; a row of unmoved pawns in front of the king sends a warning signal to watch out for possible back-rank mates, but once one of the pawns has moved, the player relaxes and it is then that mistakes occur. In the diagram position White played **33 ♗e4!** and Black resigned. The double pin has suddenly been transformed into a double attack on the enemy rooks. Neither white rook can be taken due to the back-rank mate (33...♖xa7 34 ♖xb8# and 33...♖xb5 34 ♖a8+), so one black rook must move to defend the other, but then Black loses his knight. The main line is 33...♘xf2+ 34 ♔g2 ♖ee8 35 ♖xb8 ♖xb8 36 ♔xf2 and White is a piece up.

Back-rank mate combinations often spring up unexpectedly, as in the following example.

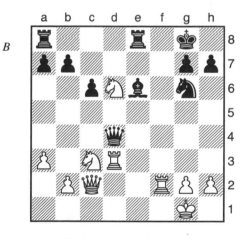

McShane – Mirumian
Lippstadt 1999

White has just played ♖e3-d3, attacking Black's queen. Since the e8-rook is also under threat, White probably expected to win material. However, Black replied with the shocking **22...♗c4!**. Although three black pieces are under attack, none of them can be captured: 23 ♘xe8 loses a piece to 23...♗xd3 followed by ...♖xe8, while 23 ♖xd4 ♖e1+ 24 ♖f1 ♖xf1# and 23 ♘xc4 ♖e1# lead to back-rank mates, the latter depending on the fact that the f2-rook is pinned. Therefore White had to play **23 ♖d1**, moving the attacked rook and at the same time covering the threatened mate on e1. However, by **23...♕xd6!** Black again exploited the weak back rank (*see diagram below*).

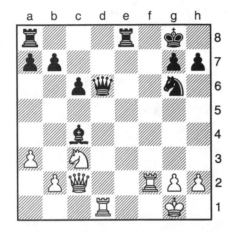

Black has won a piece for nothing, and the finish was **24 ♘e4 ♖xe4 0-1**.

Here again the lack of the traditional three-pawn line-up probably dulled White's sense of danger, although the absence of both rooks from the first rank was a warning sign that he should have heeded.

All the examples in this chapter feature kingside castling. Back-rank mates occur more often on the kingside than the queenside for two reasons. Firstly, kingside castling is in general more common than queenside castling. Secondly, queenside castling usually involves advancing the d-pawn and developing the queen's bishop; then after 0-0-0 there is a natural flight-square on d2, which makes a back-rank mate less likely. However, if White plays 0-0-0 and then ♔b1 (or ...0-0-0 followed by ...♔b8 for Black) the situation

becomes a mirror reflection of kingside castling and then back-rank mates become more likely.

Back-Rank Mate Exercises

Solutions start on page 136.

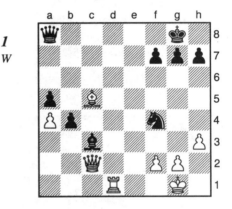

Black threatens mate in one. What should White play?

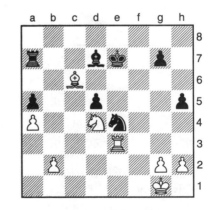

How did Black force immediate resignation?

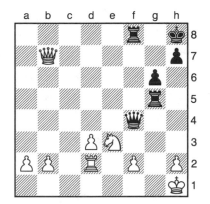

3
B

How did Black win immediately?

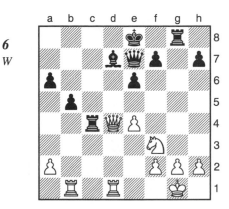

6
W

White played **24 ♕a7** and the game ended in a draw. Did he have a better move?

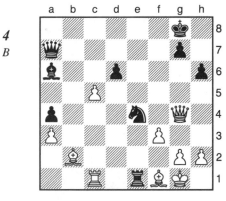

4
B

How did Black force a quick mate?

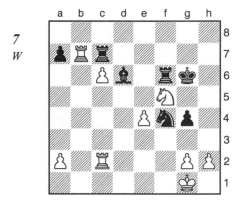

7
W

White played **43 ♘xd6** here. Why was this a mistake?

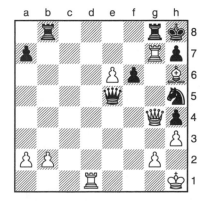

5
W

How did White push home his attack?

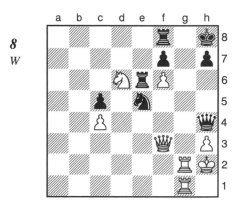

8
W

How did White exploit the back rank?

9
W

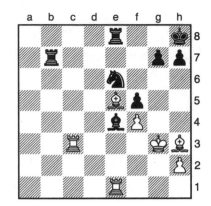

How did White win material?

11
W

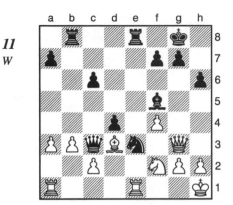

White decided to exchange bishops by **30 ♗xf5**. Was this a good idea?

10
W

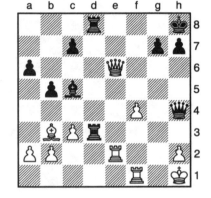

How did White force a quick win?

12
W

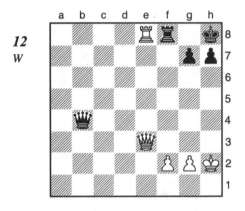

Despite the simplified position White found a forced win. What was it?

10 Pawn Promotion

When a pawn promotes to a queen, the pawn vanishes and a queen, worth nine points, appears on the board; thus the net gain is eight points. This is a large material gain and it is therefore worth a considerable sacrifice to achieve a pawn promotion.

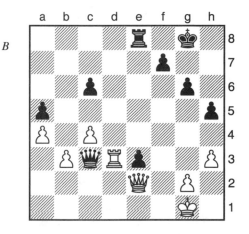

E. Berg – Ibragimov
Katrineholm 1999

This example is typical. Black has an advanced pawn, but at the moment it is blockaded by the queen. Black is willing to give up his queen for a rook (a sacrifice of four points) in order to destroy the blockade and ensure promotion, which nets him eight points within a couple of moves – a quick and profitable return on his investment. After **40...♛xd3!** White resigned since 41 ♛xd3 e2 followed by 42...e1♛+ leaves Black a whole rook up.

Pawn-promotion ideas arise frequently in the endgame, when there are more likely to be advanced pawns on the board, and there are fewer pieces around to prevent them from promoting.

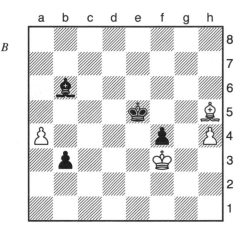

Smirin – Grishchuk
FIDE Knockout, New Delhi 2000

With equal material and opposite-coloured bishops, a draw looks likely, especially as the immediate 64...b2 can be met by 65 ♗g6, when both black pawns are halted. Even if Black can manage to play his king over to the b-pawn and win White's bishop for it, White will easily be able to capture Black's last pawn with his king. Black, however, found the subtle **64...♚f6!**. There are three ways White's bishop can cover b1 in two moves or fewer (♗f7-a2, ♗g6 and ♗g4-f5) and this sly king move covers all three. Promotion cannot be prevented and so White resigned. Note that White would have drawn had his king not been blocking the h5-d1 diagonal, for then he could have played ♗d1-c2.

When an advanced pawn is in the vicinity of the enemy king, combinations may arise which use pawn promotion as part of an attack; a new queen suddenly popping into existence will reinforce the most jaded offensive!

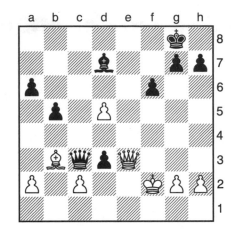

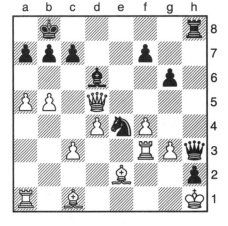

Nataf – Korchnoi
Cannes 1998

Here Black pushed home his attack with a simple but effective combination: **31...♕g2+!** and White resigned since 32 ♔xg2 h1♕# is mate. One queen vanished only to be immediately replaced by another.

The rules of chess allow a pawn to be promoted to a piece other than a queen; the other options are rook, bishop and knight. In practice, the queen is chosen the vast majority of the time because this offers the greatest material gain, but sometimes a knight is preferred, usually because a knight delivers check while a queen would not. Positions exist where a rook or bishop promotion is necessary to avoid stalemate, but these are so rare in practice that we can safely ignore them.

In the following diagram, Black is currently a pawn up, but his d3-pawn is pinned and apparently lost. However, Black found a neat combination involving promotion to a knight: **29...d2! 30 d6+** (this intermediary check doesn't change the situation) **30...♔h8** (not 30...♔f8?? 31 ♕e7#) **31 ♕xc3** (after 31

Heini Danielsen – Aagaard
Tåstrup 1999

♕e2 ♕d4+ the pawn promotes) **31...d1♘+!**. This is the point; after 31...d1♕ Black's 'combination' would have lost him a pawn, but now the knight fork nets him a piece. The diagram below shows the situation.

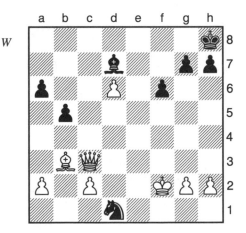

After **32 ♔e2 ♘xc3+ 33 ♔d3 b4** Black had a safe extra piece. The finish was **34 ♔d4 g5 35 ♔c5 ♘e4+ 36 ♔b6 f5 37 ♗d5 ♘xd6 38 ♔c7 ♘e8+** (Black returns the piece in order to simplify into an easily winning pawn ending) **39 ♔xd7 ♘f6+ 40 ♔e6 ♘xd5 41 ♔xd5 ♔g7 42 ♔c4 a5 43 a3 bxa3 44 ♔b3 f4 45 c4 g4 46 c5 ♔f7 0-1.**

Pawn Promotion Exercises

Solutions start on page 138.

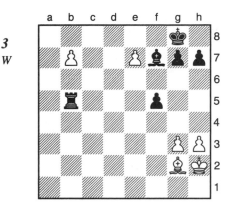

3
W

White is a rook down, but using his two passed pawns he can even win. How?

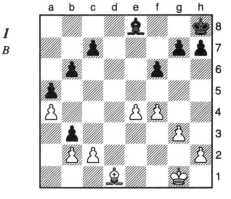

1
B

Tactics can occur even in very simplified positions. How did Black win here?

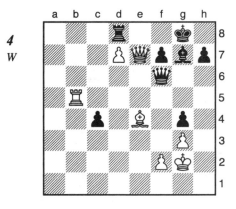

4
W

How did White force his advanced pawn home?

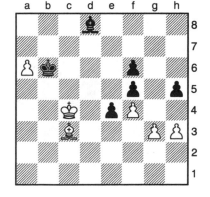

2
W

White's a-pawn looks lost. What should he play?

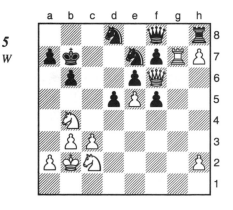

5
W

How did White win material?

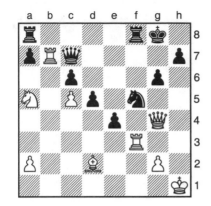

White, who is a piece up, has just played
♖b1-b7. How should Black respond?

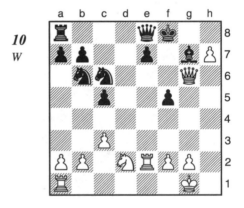

In this confusing position White is tempo-
rarily two pieces up. What should Black play?

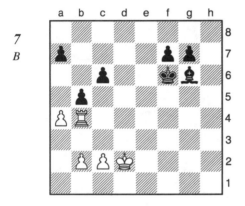

What should Black play here, 33...a6 or
33...a5?

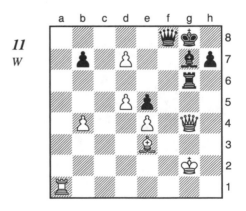

How did White exploit his advanced pawn
near the enemy king?

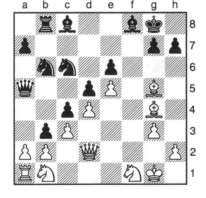

How did Black force a win?

White's queen is pinned. Should he play
42 ♗g5 or is there a better move?

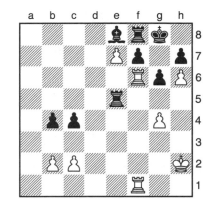

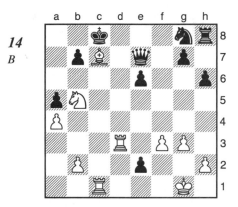

After 38 exf8♕+ White would have winning chances, but is there a better move?

White threatens 25 ♗e5+ followed by mate, or simply 25 ♘a7#. What on earth can Black do?

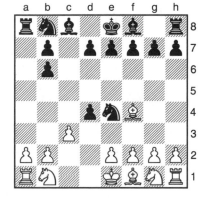

Here White played **7 ♗xb8**, with the idea of meeting 7...dxc3 by 8 ♗e5. Was this idea correct?

11 In-Between Moves

An **in-between move** (sometimes given the German name *zwischenzug*) arises when a natural sequence of moves is unexpectedly interrupted by some action taking place elsewhere. In most cases, this interruption occurs during an exchange of pieces.

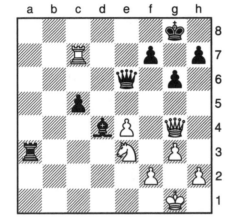

Anastasian – Annageldiev
Dubai 2001

White had just played **30 ♕f3-g4** and he now resigned without waiting for Black's reply. He had seen the sequence 30...♖xe3 31 ♕xe6 ♖e1+! (this is the in-between move; instead of recapturing the queen, which would lose the exchange, Black first of all delivers a check which safeguards his rook with gain of tempo) 32 ♔g2 (White has to reply to the check and so has no time to move his queen) 32...fxe6, when Black has won a piece.

It is very common to overlook in-between moves. When you capture a piece, it is only too natural to assume that your opponent must recapture – that is, after all, what normally

happens – only to get a rude shock when he does no such thing. This applies particularly to queen exchanges, as in the previous example.

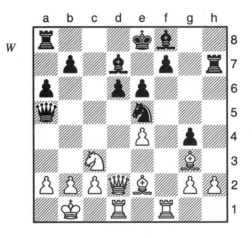

Firman – Galliamova
Moscow 2002

We have already seen the same basic arrangement of pieces in Salmensuu-Mäki (exercise 22 on page 33, where it appeared under the theme of **discovered attack**), but it is worth mentioning again as it is so common. The game continued **18 ♘d5!** (if it were not for the in-between move, then this would make no sense, since Black could simply exchange queens and then take the knight) **18...♕xd2** (there is nothing better, as White was threatening both 19 ♕xa5 and 19 ♘f6+) **19 ♘f6+** (here's the in-between move, transferring the knight to a square where it is protected; the alternative in-between move 19 ♘c7+? is wrong, as it loses a piece after 19...♔d8) **19...♔e7** (19...♔d8 loses the same way) **20 ♖xd2**. White's combination has left

Black in an untenable position. White threatens both 21 ♘xh7 and 21 ♗xe5 winning a piece (as 21...dxe5 allows 22 ♖xd7#). There is no defence against these twin threats so Black resigned.

In-between moves are especially likely to occur when there is a complex sequence of exchanges, and it pays to check carefully whether one player or the other can advantageously break away from the natural sequence.

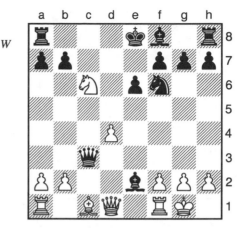

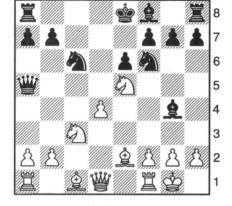

Azarov – Breder
European Under-18 Ch, Mureck 1998

Here White has just played **10 ♘f3-e5**, intending to force a general liquidation. It is easy to imagine the thoughts running through his head: "After 10...♘xe5, I play 11 dxe5 ♗xe2 12 ♕xe2 and White is better as he has a lead in development. Therefore he must play 10...♗xe2 and I reply 11 ♘xc6. If then 11...♗xd1 12 ♘xa5 I win a pawn, as both d1 and b7 are attacked. Thus Black must play 11...bxc6 and after 12 ♕xe2 the position is roughly equal." It seems that White has taken every reasonable possibility into account in his calculations, but there is an in-between move which White had not considered. The game continued **10...♗xe2 11 ♘xc6 ♕xc3!** (*see next diagram*).

Black chooses the right moment to break off the 'natural' sequence of captures and plays an unexpected move winning a piece. The end was **12 ♕xe2** (12 bxc3 ♗xd1 also costs White a piece) **12...♕xc6** (White is a piece down for nothing and could easily have resigned here) **13 ♗g5 ♗e7 14 ♖ac1 ♕d7 15 d5 ♘xd5 16 ♗xe7 ♕xe7 17 ♖fd1 ♕d7 0-1**.

The ease with which such moves can be overlooked is clear from the fact that this trap has claimed several victims, starting with Perlis (White against Tartakower) in 1907.

In-Between Moves Exercises

Solutions start on page 141.

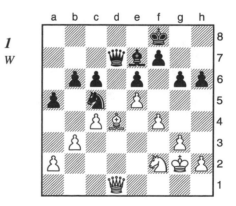

How did White win material?

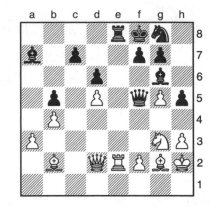

Black's queen is attacked and he continued **31...♖xe2**, counter-attacking White's queen. How did White reply?

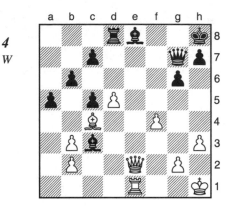

Black has just taken a knight on c3. How should White reply?

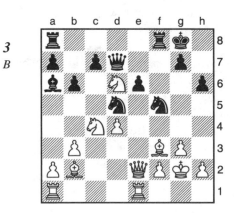

White has just taken a bishop on d6. Does Black have to recapture?

12 Defensive Tactics

In most of the examples we have seen so far, one player initiated some tactics in order to win material or force mate. However, tactics can just as well be used for defensive purposes, in order to counter threats which appear unanswerable.

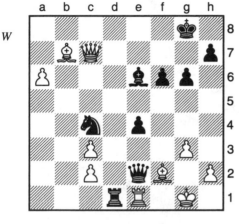

Kempinski – Gdanski
Polish Ch, Warsaw 2002

In this position Black threatens to force mate by 41...♖xe1+ 42 ♗xe1 ♕xe1+ 43 ♔g2 ♘e3#. If White plays 41 ♖xd1 ♕xd1+ 42 ♔g2, then 42...♘d2! 43 ♕d8+ ♔g7 44 ♕e7+ ♗f7 also leads to a quick mate for Black. Since White has no way of defending his e1-rook, that would appear to be the end of his resources. However, he countered Black's threats with the deflection **41 ♕d8+!**. This forks the king and the d1-rook, so Black is forced to play **41...♖xd8**. White replied **42 ♖xe2** and the tables had been turned on Black. The exchange of queens has eliminated Black's attack, and now White won easily using his advanced a-pawn: **42...e3 43**

♗xe3 ♖d1+ 44 ♔f2 ♗h3 (a last desperate attempt to mate on f1, but White easily counters it) **45 ♖e1 ♘xe3 46 ♖xd1 1-0**.

Tactics don't always work. If your opponent starts some tactics, it is important not to accept his idea at face value, but to look at it sceptically to see if it might contain a flaw.

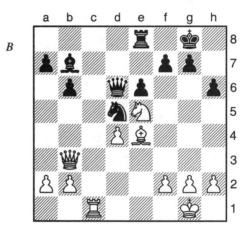

Izoria – Belov
Moscow 2002

In this position, Black suddenly unleashed the move **23...♘f4**, discovering an attack on the e4-bishop and also threatening 24...♘e2+. It would be easy for White to 'believe' Black and play a limp move such as 24 ♕e3, but in the game White put his finger on the flaw in Black's idea and played **24 ♕b5!**. This attacks the e8-rook and covers the fork on e2 with gain of tempo. Now Black is left with his bishop and rook under attack, and if 24...♖e7 (24...♖b8 is the same), then 25 ♗xb7 ♖xb7 26 ♖c8+ ♔h7 27 ♕e8 forces Black to give up his queen to avoid mate. It follows that Black cannot avoid losing material, and the game finished **24...罝d8 25 盒xb7 豐xd4** (White is simply a piece ahead) **26 罝f1 a6 27 盒xa6 罝d5 28 豐e8+ 含h7 29 ②f3 豐xb2 30 豐xf7 罝f5 31 豐b7 豐xa2 32 g3 ②h3+ 33 含g2 豐a3 34 含xh3 豐xf3 35 豐xf3 罝xf3 36 盒b7 1-0**.

There are two specific tactical ideas which by their nature can only lead to a draw, and therefore their use is restricted to situations in which one is trying to save a bad position. Some players pay less attention to drawing inferior positions than to winning favourable ones, but this is a mistake. The difference between a draw and a loss is half a point, just the same as the difference between a win and a draw. Very successful players tend not only to win a lot of games, but also to be remarkably effective at avoiding defeat. Knowledge of standard drawing ideas is very helpful in performing Houdini-like escapes from unpleasant situations.

The first of these ideas is **perpetual check**. This involves one player giving a series of checks from which there is no escape; there is no mate, but equally there is no way out and sooner or later the position is repeated, resulting in a draw.

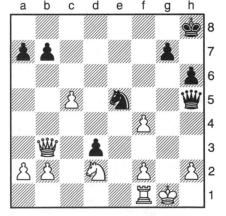

Hoffmann – Lobron
Bundesliga 2001/2

Black is a rook down, but White's king is exposed and this gives him hope for a draw. The game continued **31...豐g4+? 32 含h1 豐xf4 33 豐d5!** (now White consolidates his extra material) **33...②g4 34 豐d8+ 含h7 35 豐xd3+ 含h8 36 ②f3 含g8 37 h3 ②e5 38 ②xe5 豐xe5 39 豐e3 豐d5+ 40 含h2 豐xa2 41 豐e8+ 1-0**. However, in the diagram position Black missed a chance to force a draw. He should have played **31...②f3+!** and now **32 含h1??** 豐xh2# is mate, while after **32 含g2?** 豐g4+ 33 含h1 豐h3! 34 ②xf3 豐xf1+ 35 ②g1 d2 36 豐f7 豐d3! (not 36...d1豐 37 豐e8+! 含h7 38 豐e4+ and White gives perpetual check) Black will promote his pawn with a decisive material advantage. This means that **32 ②xf3** is forced, but after **32...豐g4+ 33 含h1 豐xf3+ 34 含g1 豐g4+** the position repeats – it is perpetual check.

Perpetual check can sometimes help to save positions which appear quite hopeless.

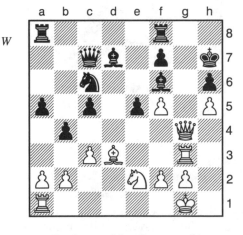

Gasiorowski – Gawronski
Darm 1994

White is a piece down for one pawn, and his threats on the kingside appear to have come to nothing. Indeed, if Black were now given a free tempo to play ...罝g8 then White would be facing inevitable defeat. All this means that if White is going to try something, then he must do so straight away. The game continued **23 ♕g7+!!** (an amazing idea; White gives up his queen in order to set up a perpetual check) **23...♗xg7 24 f6+ ♔h8** (24...♔g8 25 ♖xg7+ ♔h8 26 ♖h7+ is an immediate perpetual check) **25 ♖xg7!** (this is the key idea, threatening perpetual check on h7 and g7; 25 fxg7+? ♔g8 26 gxf8♕+ ♔xf8 is wrong as White has only a rook for the queen) **25...e4** (surprisingly, there is little Black can do to prevent the draw) **26 ♗xe4 ♖fe8** (giving the king an extra square on f8, but White forces the draw in any case) **27 ♖h7+ ♔g8 28 ♖g7+ ♔f8 29 ♖h7** (threatening mate on h8, so Black's king has to return) **29...♔g8 30 ♖g7+ ½-½**.

The second drawing tactical idea is stalemate. The rules of chess state that if you have no legal moves but your king is not under attack, then you are in **stalemate** and the game is declared drawn. Stalemate only occurs in the endgame, and although it plays an important role in the theory of certain endgames, it is easy to overlook if it arises outside one of its normal contexts.

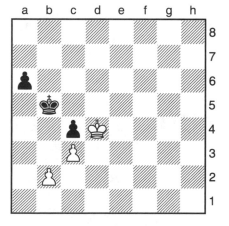

Tiviakov – I. Sokolov
Linares 1995

If Black loses his c-pawn for nothing, then the position is lost for him. A typical line is

55 ♔d5 ♔b6 56 ♔xc4 ♔c6 57 b4 ♔b6 58 ♔d5 ♔c7 59 c4 ♔d7 60 c5 ♔c7 61 c6 ♔c8 62 ♔d6 ♔d8 63 c7+ ♔c8 64 ♔c6 a5 65 b5 a4 66 b6 a3 67 b7#. Therefore White indeed played **55 ♔d5**. If Black moves his king, then White takes the c-pawn and wins, so Black replied **55...a5**. However, the continuation **56 ♔d4** put Black in a dilemma. He only has one more pawn move, 56...a4, and then 57 ♔d5 wins because now that Black's moves with his a-pawn have been exhausted, he must lose the c-pawn. Black resolved the dilemma with the move **56...♔a4!**. The threat is 57...♔b3 winning the b2-pawn, so the reply **57 ♔xc4** was forced. However, Black is now in stalemate and the game is drawn. Note that Black had to play ...a5 before playing ...♔a4, because otherwise it wouldn't have been stalemate (the king would still be able to move to a5).

In the following position Black saved the game by combining stalemate with perpetual check.

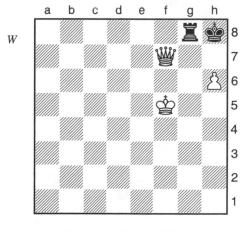

Szablewski – Radjabov
European Under-10 Ch,
Rimavska Sobota 1996

This position is winning for White, but it requires a little care. One method is 114 ♔f6 ♖g1 115 ♕a7 ♖g2 116 ♕b8+ ♖g8 117 ♕e5 (the key idea; White's queen and king are set up in such a way as to give discovered check) 117...♔h7 (if the rook moves, then White picks it up with a fork: 117...♖g2 118 ♔f7+ ♔h7 119 ♕e4+ – of course 119 ♕g7+ in this line also wins) 118 ♔f7 ♖g6 119 ♕f5 and wins. However, White actually played **114 h7?**, probably intending the line 114...♖g7 115 ♕e8+ ♔xh7 116 ♔f6 and White wins the rook in a few moves. However, Black spotted **114...♖g5+!**. If the rook is taken then it is stalemate, so White has to move his king. However, Black just follows the king, moving his rook up and down the g-file, checking all the time. There is no shelter from the checks, and if the king goes to the seventh rank, then Black plays ...♖g7, pinning and winning the white queen. The position is drawn and after the further moves **115 ♔e4 ♖g4+ 116 ♔d5 ♖g5+ 117 ♔e6 ½-½** White gave up his winning attempts.

Defensive Tactics Exercises

Solutions start on page 141.

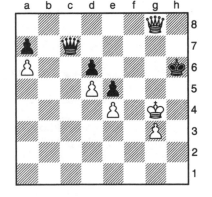

White played **66 ♔f5**. How should Black reply?

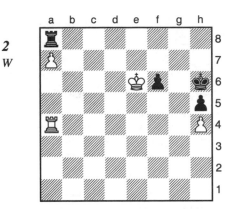

White played **58 ♔f5**. Why was this a mistake?

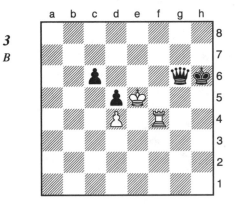

Black played a natural but bad move that allowed a draw. What was it?

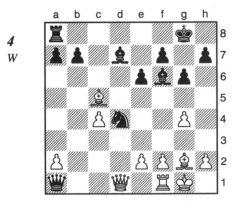

Can White, who is a piece down, trap Black's queen with **20 ♕d2?**

5
W

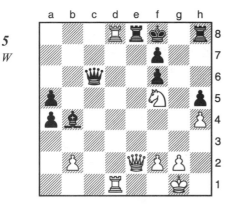

White decided to finish the game by **25 ⧨1d7**, threatening mate on e8. Does Black have anything better than resigning?

8
W

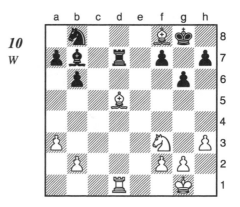

White's rook on d3 is pinned by Black's bishop. What should he play?

6
B

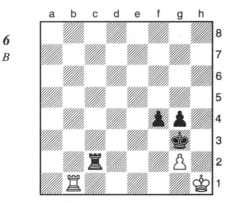

Should Black play 64...f3 or 64...⧨xg2?

9
W

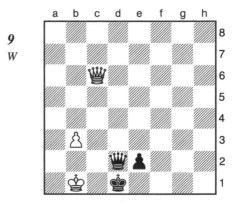

White played **69 ♕f3** and eventually lost. Did he have a better move?

7
W

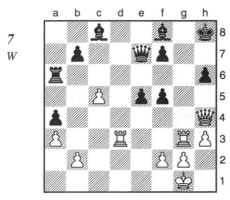

White is material down and seems to be facing defeat. How did he draw?

10
W

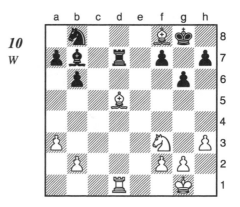

White is a piece up but both his bishops are attacked. What should he play?

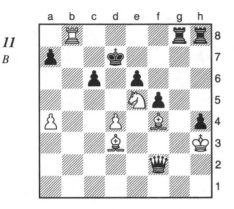

11
B

Which king move should Black play?

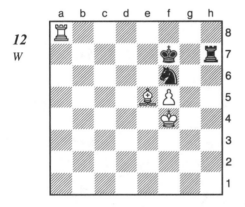

12
W

The game concluded **73 ♗xf6 ♔xf6 74 ♖a6+ ♔g7 75 ♖a7+ ♔g8 76 ♖xh7 ♔xh7 77 ♔e5 ♔g7 78 ♔e6 ♔f8 79 ♔f6 1-0**. Could Black have played better?

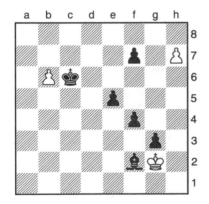

13
B

How did Black stop the h-pawn?

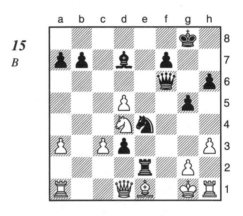

14
W

White is a piece down but 22 ♕xc7 ♘b5 favours Black. What should White play?

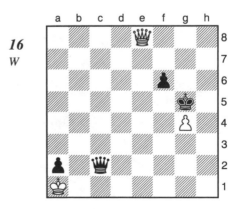

15
B

Black played **27...♘f2** and eventually lost. What should he have played instead?

16
W

White should White play in this awkward position?

13 Combinations

In the early chapters of this book, we looked at the basic tactical elements. Later chapters dealt with more advanced topics, and now we focus exclusively on situations in which the winning idea depends on two or more tactical elements. In this book we use the word 'combination' to describe such situations but, as with many chess terms, there is no generally accepted definition of 'combination' and you should be aware that other authors may use this word in a different sense. Since the various tactical elements can be combined in countless different ways, this topic is quite open-ended and we will only be able to look at a small fraction of the possibilities.

There is no clear dividing line between a 'tactic' and a 'combination', since there is a whole spectrum of difficulty from one-move tactics to massively complex multi-move combinations. The following position is an example of a simple idea which nevertheless depends on two tactical elements.

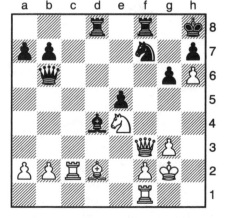

Keitlinghaus – Kummerow
Recklinghausen 1997

Here the black queen must defend f6, otherwise White could mate by ♕f6+ followed by ♕g7#. This naturally gives rise to the idea of a deflection, and indeed White played 27 ♗a5!, winning the exchange. After 27...♕e6 28 ♗xd8 Black resigned since 28...♖xd8 29 ♖c7 costs him further material. Here the skewer element of the combination was vital, because if Black's d8-rook had been, say, on e8 then ♗a5 would not have been decisive.

Not surprisingly, it is the basic tactical elements (pin, fork, skewer, deflection) which are most often linked in combinations.

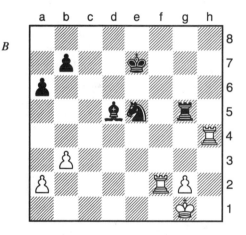

Shirov – Salov
Wijk aan Zee 1998

In this position Black won by **36...♘f3+ 0-1**, with the combination of pin and fork netting him the exchange for nothing.

As combinations become more complicated, there is a greater chance of them being missed in over-the-board play.

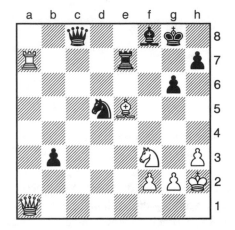

Peng Zhaoqin – Krasenkow
Wijk aan Zee 2002

White has just unwisely played **37 ♗g3-e5?**. The fact that White's queen must defend the rook on a7 suggests a possible deflection, but the obvious ...b2 seems to have been prevented by White's last move. Despite this, Black played **37...b2!**, based on the unexpected fork 38 ♗xb2 ♛b8+ winning the rook. The game ended **38 ♛a2 b1♛ 39 ♛xd5+ ♛e6 0-1**. Here White's bishop had been on the h2-b8 diagonal for some time, and so there had been no possibility of a check on this diagonal. When it did arise, White overlooked it.

In this case, no fewer than three tactical elements are necessary for the combination to work. How does one spot the winning idea? Very often the key is to focus on a potential weakness, and see what is necessary to exploit it. The line g3-b8 leading to Black's king strikes the eye, and indeed if White's knight were not there he would be able to play the discovered check e6+. It is true that Black would be able to meet this by ...♛c7, but then the pin ♗f4 would be decisive. In order for this to work, White only needs to get rid of the knight with gain of tempo, and this explains the motivation behind **23 ♘xg6!**. This not only captures a pawn, but also attacks the h8-rook, so whether Black takes the knight or not he faces a considerable loss of material; Black therefore resigned. In this example a chain of logic led White to find ♘xg6, which forced victory using line-opening, discovered check and pin.

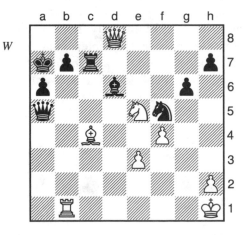

Lautier – V. Milov
Biel 1997

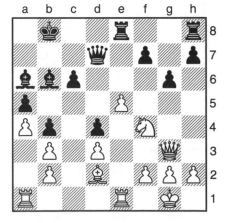

S. Movsesian – B. Lalić
Olympiad, Elista 1998

Here Black has just played **40...♗c5-d6?**, overlooking White's threat. After the fork **41 ♘c6+!** Black faced loss of his queen, since the rook and b7-pawn are both pinned, the latter due to mate on b8. After **41...♖xc6 42 ♛xa5** Black resigned. How is it that Black, a strong grandmaster, managed to overlook White's combination? It can only be explained by the fact that the c6-square appears well-defended, with two black pieces covering it, and this visual impression is so strong that Black did not even consider the check on c6. Had he done so, he surely would have noticed that both defences are nullified by pins.

Such 'visual' errors are surprisingly common, even amongst very strong players.

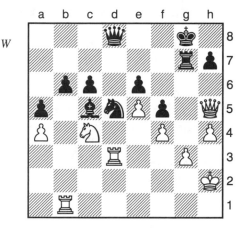

Goldin – Sapunov
Russian Ch, St Petersburg 1998

Here Black has just played **34...b7-b6?**, which probably seemed like a good idea. White was attacking the b7-pawn with his rook, and Black advanced it to a square where it is defended three times (34...♗b4 was better). The reply **35 ♘xb6!** must have been a shock. The problem is that the d5-knight is pinned, while Black's queen cannot move to b6 due to ♕e8#. Thus two of the three defenders are not really defending b6 at all. That leaves just the bishop to cope with two white attackers, a woefully inadequate defence. Black could have limped on by 35...♗b4, but as he would have been the whole exchange down he would not have had any hope of saving the game. He therefore resigned immediately.

Khuzman – Kasparov
European Clubs Cup, Rethymnon 2003

In this position one of the greatest players of all time continued **20...♗c8?**, trying to drive White's knight away from the active f5-square. With his d5-pawn defended three times and only attacked once, it probably seemed to Kasparov that he could afford to remove one of the defenders. White's shocking reply **21 ♖xd5!** exposed the flaw in Black's logic. The first point is that f6-knight isn't really defending the d5-pawn because it is pinned against the mate on g7. However, there is worse to come: Black's queen isn't genuinely defending the d5-pawn either, because if it moves to d5 then White can win the queen by the fork ♘e7+. Thus, despite the visual appearance of secure defence, the d5-pawn has only one effective defender, the bishop, and that is precisely the piece which Kasparov mistakenly moved away. The game continued **21...♕e8 22 ♗xc4** and here Black resigned, since he is two pawns down for no compensation. If Kasparov can fall victim to this sort of oversight, then anybody can!

Another common reason for overlooking a combination is that the position appears so quiet that it is hard to imagine any tactics occurring, and so the player doesn't bother to look for them.

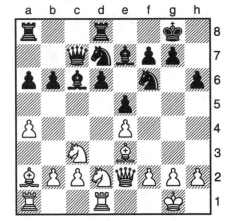

Van den Doel – Gormally
London 1998

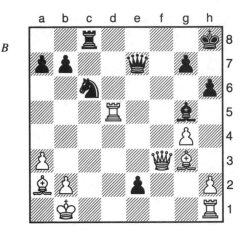

Antić – Abramović
Yugoslav Ch, Banja Koviljaca 2002

Black has just played **15...♖f8-d8?** and it is hard to imagine that this is a fatal error. However, by combining a fork and a pin, White forced a material gain. He played **16 ♕c4!**, attacking the f7-pawn (which Black weakened with his previous move). The only way to defend this pawn is by 16...♖f8, but then comes 17 ♘d5, forking the queen and the e7-bishop. Black's queen also has the duty of defending the c6-bishop, so 17...♘xd5 is forced, but after 18 exd5 Black loses a piece thanks to the pin along the c-file.

Our final example is a combination which blends several elements and defies categorization.

Black sacrificed a rook to reach the position in the following diagram and at first sight he doesn't seem to have much for it. True, there is an advanced pawn on the seventh rank, but the promotion square is covered by two white pieces. Black justified his play with the remarkable move **25...♘d4!!**. This attacks White's queen, but there is a deadly second threat: 26...e1♕+ 27 ♖xe1 ♕xe1+ (sacrificing two queens!) 28 ♗xe1 ♖c1#. So far we have seen line-opening (the c-file), line-closing (the d-file) removing the

guard and back-rank mate, but there is also a fork after 26 ♕f2 ♕e4+. White cannot avoid loss of material and the game finished: **26 ♖xd4 e1♕+! 27 ♕d1** (27 ♖xe1 ♕xe1+ 28 ♗xe1 ♖c1#) **27...♕xd1+ 28 ♖hxd1 ♗f6 29 ♖c4 ♖xc4 30 ♗xc4 ♕e4+ 31 ♗d3 ♕xg4 32 ♖e1 g5 33 ♗e4 ♕d7 34 ♗f2 ♕d2 0-1.**

Combinations Exercises

Solutions start on page 144.

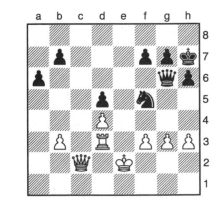

1
B

How did Black win using a pin and a fork?

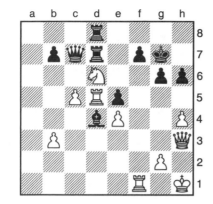

2
W

What has Black overlooked?

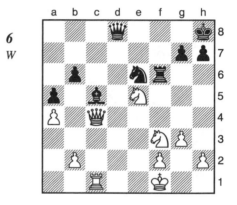

5
B

How did Black force a win here?

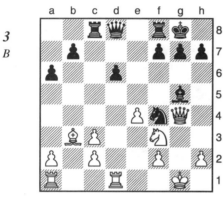

3
B

Black's bishop is attacked. What should he play?

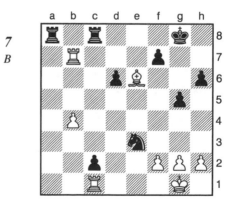

6
W

How did White finish the game at a stroke?

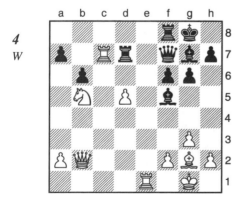

4
W

Which tactical elements did White combine to force a win?

How did Black exploit his advantage?

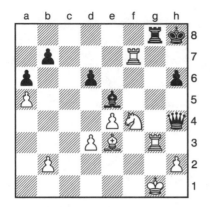

8
W

White is down on material and seems set to lose. How did he turn the tables?

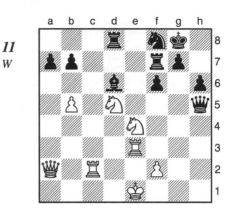

11
W

White won in spite of being three pawns down. How?

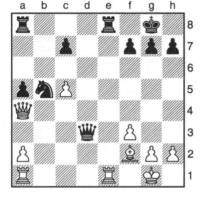

9
W

White found a forced win. What was it?

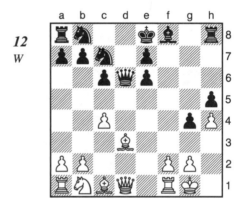

12
W

White has few pieces developed, but despite this he found a lethal blow. What was it?

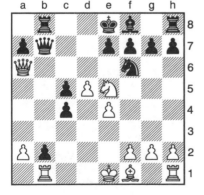

10
W

How did White push his attack home?

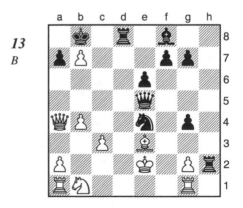

13
B

White has the deadly threat of 21 ♕xa7+. What should Black play?

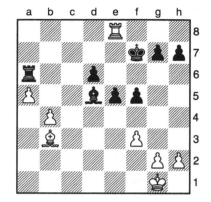

14
W

White's rook and bishop are both attacked. How should he continue?

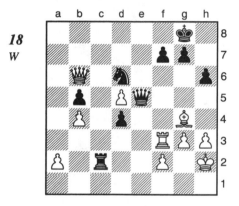

17
W

How did White gain material?

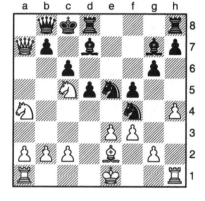

15
W

How did White win quickly?

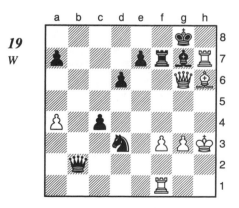

18
W

How did White win material with a small combination?

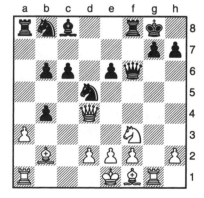

16
W

How did White win material?

19
W

How did White force his attack home?

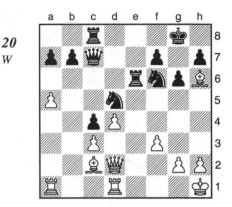

20
W

How did White win material?

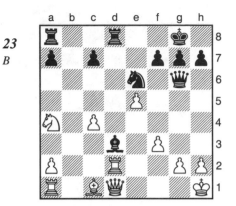

23
B

How did Black win material?

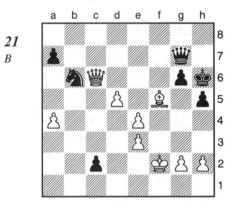

21
B

Black's queen appears to be tied down to the mate threat on g6. How did he overcome this and win?

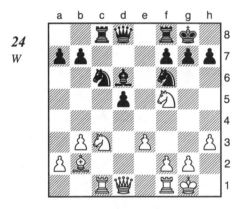

24
W

Black resigned after White's next move. What was it?

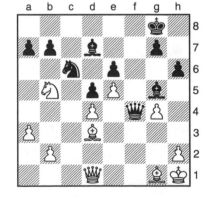

22
B

How did Black exploit White's cornered king to win?

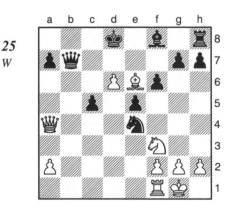

25
W

How did White exploit Black's exposed king?

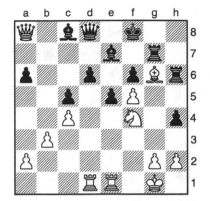

26
W

How did White break through Black's wall of pawns?

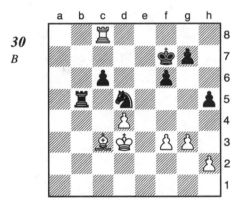

29
B

How did Black win material?

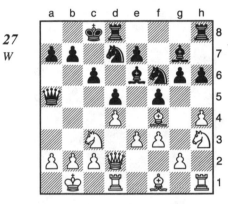

27
W

What is White's strongest continuation?

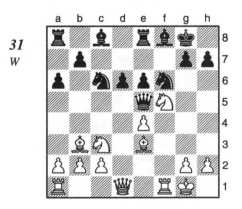

30
B

Black's c6-pawn is under attack. What should he play?

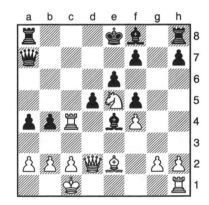

28
W

How did White score a quick win?

31
W

Two moves were enough to secure White a decisive material advantage. What were they?

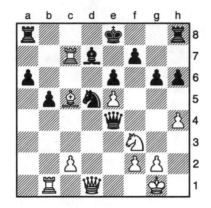

32
W

What was the combination that secured the win for White here?

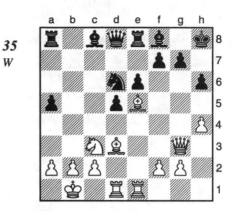

35
W

How did White win with an unexpected combination?

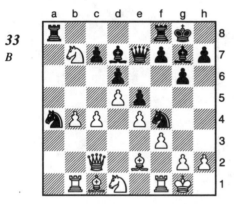

33
B

How did Black win material?

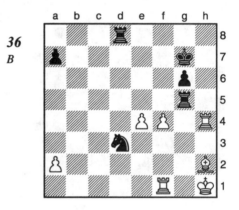

36
B

The position doesn't look ripe for a tactical finish, but appearances can be deceptive. How did Black win?

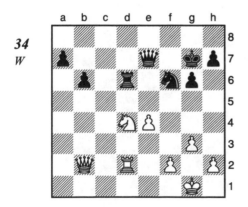

34
W

White found a forcing continuation that won material. What was it?

14 Miscellaneous Exercises

The following exercises include examples of all the tactical themes covered in this book. However, no clue is given as to the theme or difficulty of each exercise. Your objective is to find the best move in each position. Normally that means finding a winning move, but in three positions you have to find a drawing resource in a bad position. Good luck!

Solutions start on page 149.

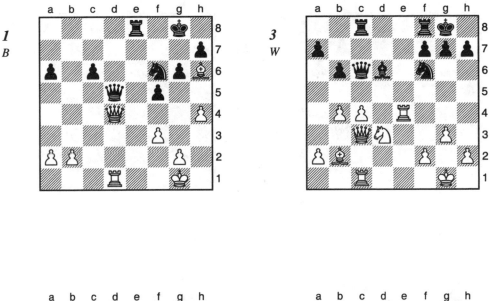

1
B

3
W

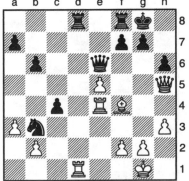

2
B

4
B

5
W

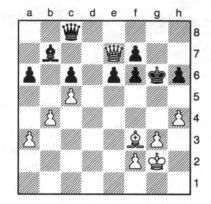

8
W

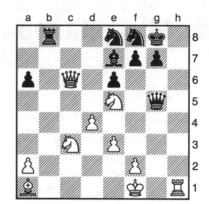

6
W

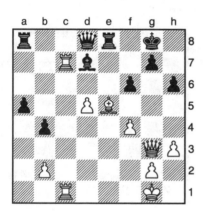

9
B

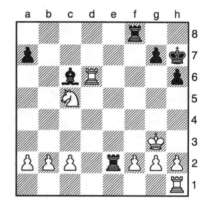

7
B

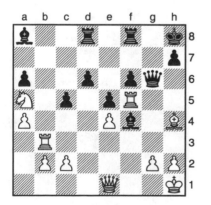

10
W

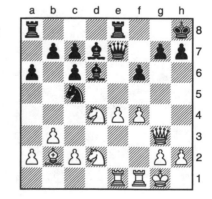

11
B

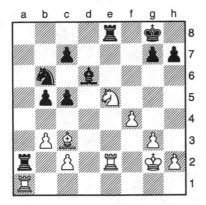

14
B

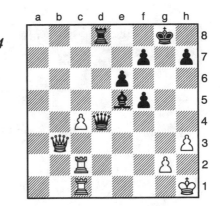

12
W

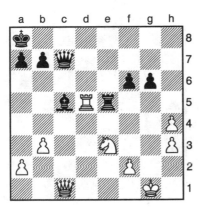

15
B

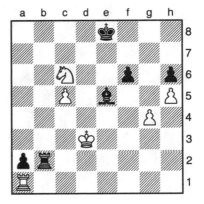

13
W

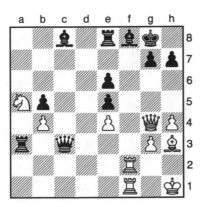

16
W

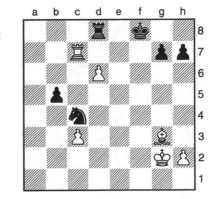

17
W

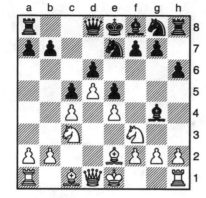

20
B

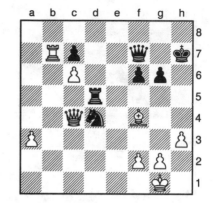

18
B

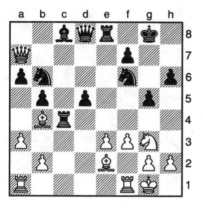

21
W

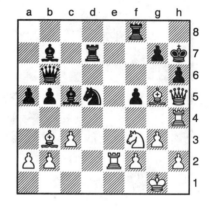

19
B

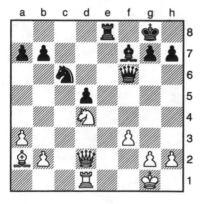

22
B

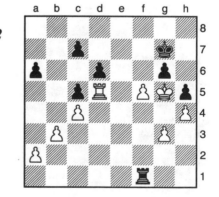

23
W

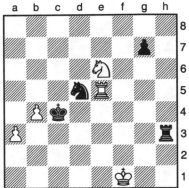

26
B

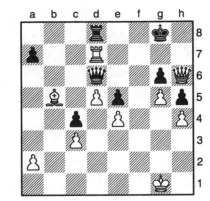

24
B

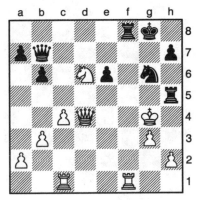

27
W

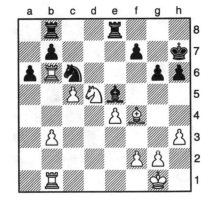

25
W

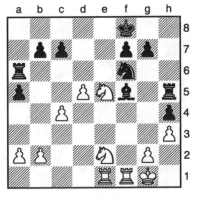

28
W

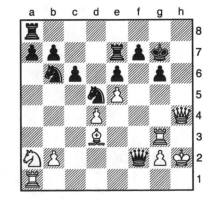

29
B

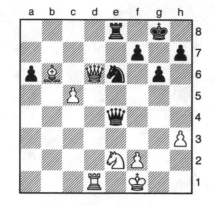

32
B

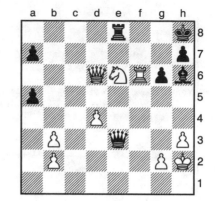

30
W

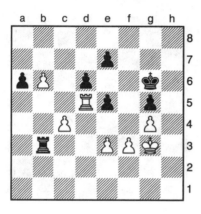

33
B

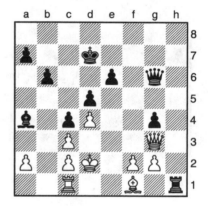

31
B

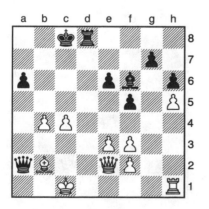

34
W

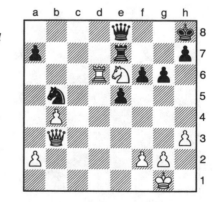

35
B

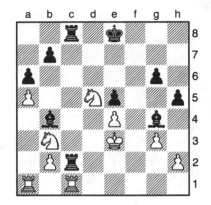

38
W

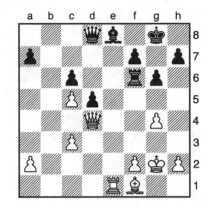

36
W

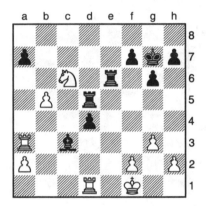

39
W

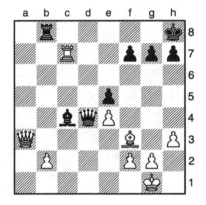

37
B

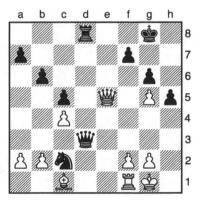

40
W

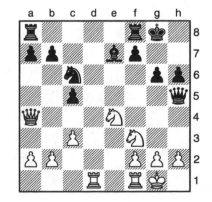

41
W

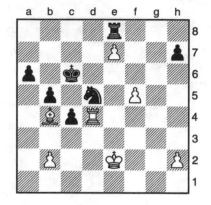

44
W

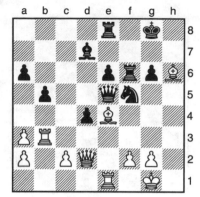

42
W

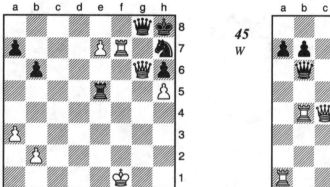

45
W

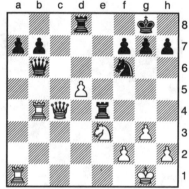

43
W

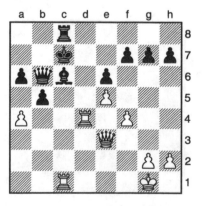

46
B

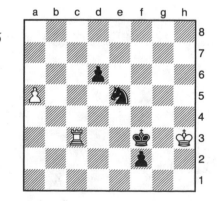

47
W

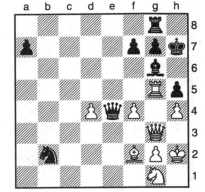

48
W

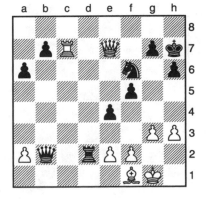

49
B

50
W

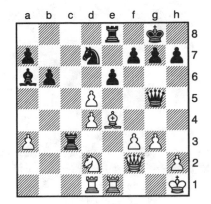

51
B

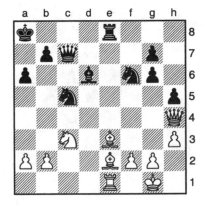

52
B

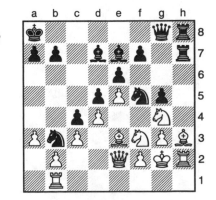

53
B

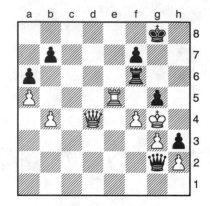

56
B

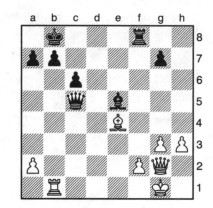

54
B

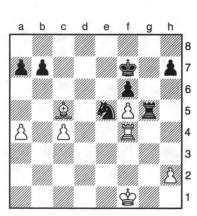

57
W

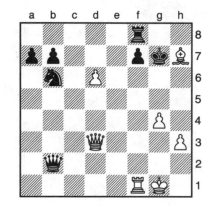

55
B

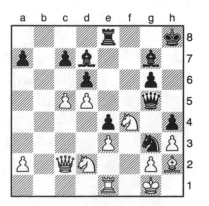

58
W

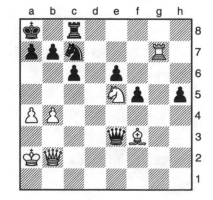

59
B

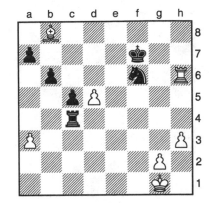

62
B

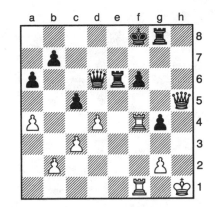

60
W

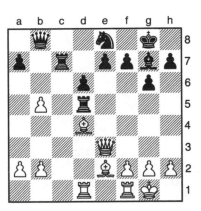

63
W

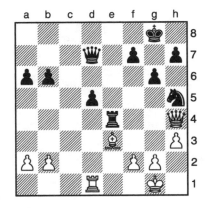

61
W

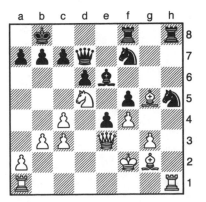

64
B

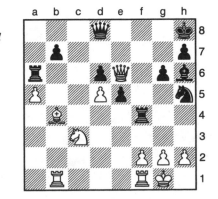

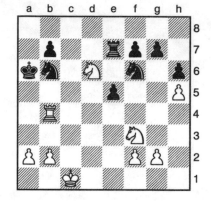

65
W

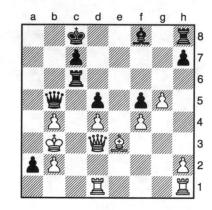

66
B

Solutions

Solutions to Fork Exercises

1)

Papaioannou – Mastrovasilis
Greek Ch, Athens 1998

White won by **77 ♘f4+ 1-0**, picking up the bishop with a knight fork.

2)

Vallejo Pons – Avrukh
Olympiad, Istanbul 2000

No, it wasn't. Black replied **25...♖c5** winning a piece by forking the undefended bishop and knight. White fought on but was forced to concede in the end: **26 ♗d3 ♖xe5 27 f4 ♖c5 28 f5 ♗c8 29 e5 ♘e8 30 g4 ♔f8 31 ♖ab1 ♘c6 32 ♖b5 f6 33 exf6 ♗xf6 34 d7 ♗d4+ 35 ♔f1 ♗xd7 36 ♖xb7 ♗c8 0-1**.

3)

Sutovsky – Dizdar
European Team Ch, Pula 1997

The simple **38 ♘f4+** forked king and rook. Black resigned at once since after 38...♔g5 39 ♘xh5 ♔xh5 40 ♖xg7 he is well down on material and his king is cut off on the edge of the board.

4)

S. Buckley – Lane
British Ch, Torquay 2002

White's last move was to push his pawn from e4 to e5. Black exploited this mistake by **26...♕c5+**, forking king and bishop and winning a piece for nothing. The game ended **27 ♔h1 ♕xd5 28 ♖d1 ♕g8 29 ♕xf4 ♖xb2 30 ♕h4 ♖xd1 31 ♖xd1 ♗b7 0-1**.

5)

Abramović – Tischbierek
European Clubs Cup, Berlin 1996

White's queen and rook are lined up on the same diagonal so Black played **23...♗e2** and White resigned since he is losing at least a piece.

6)

Vaganian – Mikhalevski
Vlissingen 1999

The undefended a4-bishop and the exposed black king are clear pointers to the danger of a fork. White played **25 ♕c4+** winning a piece, and Black immediately resigned. Note that 25 ♖xd8 ♕xd8 26 ♕c4+ is equally effective.

7)

Vaulin – Smagin
Russian Ch (rapid playoff), Elista 1997

No, it wasn't a good idea because White now played **9 ♕e5+** winning the knight on b8. Undefended pieces can be a weakness even in the opening. Black limped on a piece down before resigning on move 23.

8)

Levitt – Golod
MSO Masters, London 1999

After **20...♘c4** Black's knight is attacking White's queen and e3-bishop. White's queen cannot move so as to defend the bishop, so he loses a piece for nothing. White resigned at once.

9)

M. Gurevich – Van der Sterren
Zonal tournament, Escaldes 1998

Black resigned after **24 ♖d6**, as his queen and knight are forked. He can try 24...♕f7, attacking the f4-bishop, but White wins a piece in any case after 25 ♗xd5 ♕xf4 26 ♖xb6.

10)

Halkias – Fouad
Tanta City 2002

White played **27 ♖xb7** and Black resigned, since he loses a piece after 27...♖xb7 28 ♕c8+ followed by ♕xb7.

11)

Smirnov – Ionov
Russian Ch, Samara 2000

Black played **14...♘b4**, which threatens both 15...♘xd5 and the second knight fork 15...♘xa2+. White must lose material, the main line being 15 ♖a5 ♕xa5 16 ♘xa5 ♘xa2+ followed by 17...♘xc3 winning the exchange. The game actually concluded **15 ♕c5 ♘xd5 16 ♕xd5 ♗e6 17 ♕h5 ♕xf2 18 ♗d3 ♕e3+ 19 ♘d2 g6 20 ♕h4 ♖ac8 21 ♔d1 ♗d5 0-1**.

12)

Kramnik – Kasparov
BGN World Ch (game 2), London 2000

Black resigned after the decisive **40 ♗d5** since there is no reply to the twin threats of 41 ♗xa2 and 41 ♖e6+, picking up Black's bishop.

13)

Zacharias – Hasenbank
Hamburg 1999

Once again we see that tactics can be very important in the endgame. After **52...♘d7** Black threatens mate on f6, but the only move to prevent mate, 53 ♔g4, loses the bishop to the fork 53...♘f6+. White actually preferred a quick death by **53 ♗c6 ♘f6# (0-1)**.

14)

Holusova – Pardy
Ostrava 2002

After **30...♖xd3** White resigned since 31 ♖xd3 ♕b1+ followed by ...♕xd3 leaves Black a rook up.

15)

Cummins – Eichab
Olympiad, Bled 2002

White probably expected Black to retreat his queen to c5, but instead Black won a piece with a typical tactical blow involving a knight fork: **19...♕xc3! 20 ♕xc3 ♘e2+ 21 ♔f1 ♘xc3**. White struggled on but eventually had to resign.

16)

Barsov – Sharma
Calcutta 2001

The preliminary sacrifice **34 ♖d7+!** deflected Black's queen onto the right square for a knight fork. After **34...♕xd7 35 ♘e5+ ♔e8 36 ♘xd7 ♔xd7 37 ♕xg7+ ♔d6 38 ♕xh6** White had a decisive material advantage and won quickly: **38...♖g8 39 f3 ♔e7 40 ♕h7+ ♔f8 41 ♕h6+ ♔f7 42 ♕f4+ ♔f6 43 e4 ♗c6 44 ♕h6+ ♔f7 45 exf5 ♗d5 46 fxe6+ ♗xe6 47 ♕f4+ ♔e7 48 ♕e5 ♔f7 49 ♔f2 1-0**.

17)

Nanu – Sanduleac
Calimanesti 1999

The game concluded **33 ♖bxc5** and Black resigned because 33...dxc5 34 d6+ ♔d7 35 ♖xc7+ leaves White a piece up for just one pawn.

18)

de Firmian – Kobaliya
FIDE Knockout, Las Vegas 1999

Black is a pawn up in any case, but he found a clean kill with **57...♕xe3!** and White resigned, since 58 ♕xe3 ♘xg4+ 59 ♔g3 ♘xe3 leaves Black a piece and two pawns up.

19)

Zontakh – Martinović
Belgrade 2000

After **25 ♖xe7! ♖xe7 26 ♕f6+** Black resigned as White will continue with ♕xe7, winning a piece for nothing.

20)

Jenni – Züger
Swiss Ch, Leukerbad 2002

White resigned after the queen sacrifice **40...♕xf5!**. If 41 ♕xf5, then 41...♘d4+ followed by 42...♘xf5 wins a piece, while after 41 ♕xc6 e3+ (a **discovered check** – see Chapter 2) 42 ♔c1 (or 42 ♔b2 ♕e5+ 43 ♔a2 e2 and the pawn promotes) 42...exf2 White has only a few checks and then the f2-pawn promotes with check: 43 ♕e8+ ♔b7 44 ♕e7+ ♔a6 or 43 ♕d6+ ♔b7 44 ♕e7+ ♔a6.

21)

A. Kovačević – Pavlović
Yugoslav Ch, Herceg Novi 2001

A preliminary sacrifice set up a fork along the long diagonal: **48 ♖f5+ ♔e6 49 ♖xd5** and Black resigned since 49...♔xd5 (49...♖e1+ 50 ♔d4 defends the rook) 50 ♗e4+ followed by ♗xh1 leaves White a piece and a pawn up for nothing.

22)

Adams – Timman
Dortmund 1999

Unusually, White managed to arrange a king fork after **41 ♖xf6+! ♔xf6 42 ♔d5**. Black's rook and bishop are attacked, and the rook has no move to keep guarding the bishop. If he plays 42...♖c8, then 43 ♔xd6 is an easy win for White since not only has he two pieces for a rook, but Black's pawns are ready to drop off, starting with the one on c5. Black therefore preferred **42...♗f4 43 ♔xc6 ♗xd2**, but **44 ♘xc5** left him a pawn down with a very bad position. The finish was **44...♔e5 45 b4!** and Black resigned, since 45...♗xb4 46 ♘d3+ is another fork, while

otherwise White wins by pushing his queenside pawns.

23)

Yagupov – Najer
Linares open 2001

In the endgame an extra pawn often proves decisive. Here Black continued **39...♕xf1+! 40 ♔xf1 ♘xh2+ 41 ♔e2 ♘xf3 42 ♔xf3** with an easy win in prospect since he can make an outside passed pawn on the h-file. The game ended **42...g5 43 ♔e4 ♔g6 0-1**; the finish might be 44 f4 (44 ♔e5 f5 followed by ...h4) 44...h4 45 gxh4 gxh4 46 ♔f3 ♔f5 47 ♔e3 ♔g4, etc.

24)

Schmied – Ammer
Vienna 1996

The diagram position arose after the moves **1 e4 e5 2 ♗c4 ♗c5 3 ♘f3 d6 4 d3 ♗g4**. White was now tempted by the sacrifice **5 ♗xf7+?**, but the combination is unsound.

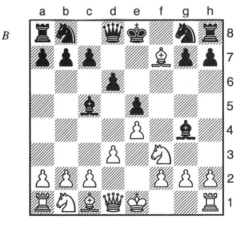

After 5...♔xf7, White has two possible continuations, but neither works. If 6 ♘xe5+ dxe5 7 ♕xg4, then White has given up two pieces to win one, and so ends up a piece down. 6 ♘g5+ may appear more promising, since if Black moves his king then White can play 7 ♕xg4, ending up with an extra pawn.

However, the surprising reply 6...♕xg5! 7 ♗xg5 ♗xd1 8 ♔xd1 again leaves Black a piece up. In the game, however, Black played **5...♔d7??** and soon resigned: **6 ♘xe5+ dxe5 7 ♕xg4+ ♔e7 8 ♕xg7 1-0**. There are two important lessons to be learnt here. Firstly, even if you spot a familiar pattern, the specifics of the combination still need to be checked; and secondly, you shouldn't believe your opponent – his combination may not be correct.

25)

Landa – Shipov
Russian Ch, St Petersburg 1998

After **24...♗e4!** Black wins material. The f3-rook is attacked and cannot move away because it is pinned by the e4-bishop. Thus **25 ♖xe4** is the only way to prevent the capture of the f3-rook, but then **25...♕g6+ 26 ♔h2 ♕xe4** wins the other rook. Black is now a pawn up and has a positional advantage because White's kingside pawns are weak. In the game he won quickly: **27 ♖e3 ♕b4 28 ♖d3 ♖xd3 29 cxd3 ♗c5 30 d4 ♗d6 31 ♔g2 ♕a5 32 f5 ♕xa2 33 d5 ♕xb3 34 dxc6 bxc6 35 f6 ♕d5+ 36 ♔f1 0-1**.

26)

Sorokin – Giaccio
Argentine Ch, Buenos Aires 1998

Yes, after **32 ♕c8+** White wins far more than a mere pawn. Black resigned as he loses a whole rook after 32...♔h7 33 ♕xf5+, forking king and rook.

27)

Bakhtadze – Arbakov
Russia Cup, Moscow 1999

Black spotted the possibility of a fork on e5 and played **29...♗xe5**. The continuation was **30 b4** (after 30 fxe5 ♕xe5+ Black wins two pawns and the exchange, so White tries to force the black queen to lose contact with the e5-square) **30...♕d6 31 c5 ♕c7** (White's attempts have failed and now he faces the loss of a second pawn) **32 ♖f1 ♗xf4 33 ♖h4**

♕e5+ **34 ♔d1 ♖xh5 35 ♖hxf4 f5 36 ♖4f2 ♕e3 37 ♔c2 ♖h3 0-1**. If 38 ♕xe3 dxe3 the pawn fork costs White more material.

28)

Anastasian – Stojanovski
World Team Ch, Erevan 2001

After **33 ♖xc7!** (White should not try to play his moves in reverse order, since 33 ♖d8+? can be met by 33...♘e8) Black resigned as 33...♖xc7 34 ♖d8+ ♔g7 35 ♘e6+ followed by ♘xc7 leaves him a piece down for nothing.

29)

Abatino – Skembris
Cutro 1999

Black continued **20...♖d2** and White resigned immediately. The threat is 21...♕c2+ 22 ♔a1 ♕xb2# (or 22...♕c1#) and if 21 ♕xe4 then 21...♖d1#. The only other possibility is 21 ♗xd2, but then the fork comes into play by 21...♘xd2+ followed by 22...♘xf3.

30)

Moradiabadi – Adianto
Asian Ch, Calcutta 2001

Black is just a pawn up, but finished the game with the single stroke **60...♗xf2!**, and White immediately resigned. After 61 ♕xf2 ♕xe4+ White's king and knight are forked and he will be left three pawns down.

31)

Rajlich – Lputian
New York 1998

There is a potential knight fork on e2, which Black realised by **21...♕xc1! 22 ♘xc1** (22 ♕xc1 ♘xe2+ is also hopeless for White) **22...♖xc1**. Here White resigned because his queen is pinned and 23 ♕xc1 runs into 23...♘xe2+. However White plays, he ends up at least a rook down. Note that if Black plays for a **back-rank mate** (a mate with rook or queen on the first rank – see Chapter 9) by 21...♘xe2+ 22 ♕xe2 ♕xc1+ 23 ♘xc1

♖xc1+, then White can defend by means of 24 ♘f1.

32)

Belov – Nikitin
Russia Cup, Moscow 1999

This is a case of **removing the guard** (see Chapter 7). By destroying the bishop on d7, White sets up a fork on e6. The game ended **21 ♖xd7! ♖xd7 22 ♘xe6 ♛b6** (in addition to the e6-pawn, Black will also lose the one on f5) **23 ♘xf8 ♗xf8 24 ♛xf5** (White is two pawns up and moreover Black's position is completely shattered; his rook is pinned and his bishop and e5-knight are under attack) **24...♗d6 25 ♖d1 ♚c7 26 c4 1-0**. There is no answer to the threats of 27 c5 and 27 ♖xd6.

33)

Aronian – Beshukov
Hastings 2000/1

White ignored the mate threat and won a rook by **26 ♘f6+ ♚g7** (26...♚h8 27 ♛xf8#) **27 ♛xf8+! ♚xf8** (27...♚xf6 28 ♛h8#) when Black resigned without waiting for 28 ♘xh7+ followed by ♘xg5.

34)

Zakharov – Alavkin
Russia Cup, Novgorod 1997

The sacrifice **19 ♖xe4!** proved decisive. After 19...dxe4 20 ♛xe4 White is threatening both 21 ♛xa8+ and 21 ♛xh7+ ♚f8 22 ♛h8+ ♚e7 23 ♘g6#. There is no reasonable defence to the twin threats; e.g., 20...♖ff8 21 ♛xh7+ ♚f7 22 ♛xg7+ ♚e8 23 ♗g6+ and mate in two more moves. Black therefore declined the sacrifice by **19...♗d6**, but after **20 ♖e2 ♗xe5 21 ♖xe5** White was a piece up and Black resigned.

35)

Schiller – Yakovich
New York 1998

The preliminary exchange **31 ♗xc5** (31 ♛xd3? is ineffective owing to 31...♗xb6)

31...♘xc5 set up Black's knight for a fork by the white queen. After **32 ♛e8+ ♚g7** (Black also loses the knight after 32...♚h7 33 ♛xf7+ ♚h8 34 ♛f8+) **33 ♛e5+** Black resigned as he loses the knight for nothing.

36)

Gunnarsson – Slobodian
European Ch, Ohrid 2001

No, White has a much stronger move than simply recapturing on b3. He played **21 ♘ef6+! gxf6 22 ♖xe8+ ♛xe8 23 ♘xf6+** and Black resigned as he will end up with only two minor pieces for his queen.

37)

Acs – Ovseevich
Budapest 1999

White won a piece with the fork **35 ♛a5**, which threatens both 36 ♛xa4 and 36 ♖xa8. Black replied **35...♖xa6**, but after **36 ♛xa6** there is again a fork, this time of the a4-knight and the c8-rook. Black therefore resigned.

38)

Marchand – Guidarelli
Paris 2002

Black won material with a very attractive combination based on consecutive knight forks. He played **31...♛f3+!** (a queen sacrifice sets up the following knight charge) **32 ♛xf3 ♘xh4+** (the first knight fork) **33 ♚f1 ♘xf3** and unfortunately for White he falls victim to a second knight fork in a row. After **34 ♖ed1 ♘xd2+ 35 ♖xd2 ♗e5 36 ♚e2 ♖g7** White resigned rather than play on a rook down.

39)

Lautier – Karlsson
Malmö 1999

A preliminary check is necessary to drive Black's king into the right position for a later g6+ to set up a fork. The game finished **40 ♖d8+!** (40 g6? is less good because after

40...♘e3+! 41 ♘xe3 fxe3 42 fxe3 ♖a4 43 ♖h7+ ♔g8 44 ♖xh5 ♔g7 White will still have to do some work to win the ending) 40...♔h7 41 ♖xd5! (41 g6+! ♔xg6 42 ♖xd5 ♖xd5 43 ♘e7+ is also effective) 1-0. After 41...♖xd5 42 g6+ Black will sooner or later have to put his king on g6 or g8, allowing a fork on e7; for example, 42...♔h8 43 g7+ ♔h7 44 g8♕+ ♔xg8 45 ♘e7+ and White will be a whole piece ahead.

40)

Cifuentes – Spraggett

Ampuriabrava 1997

White is a pawn down and although he can regain it by 51 ♘xe6+ ♘xe6 52 ♕xe6, he could not hope for more than a draw after 52...♖d4. Instead, White found the surprising 51 ♕xe6!. If Black takes the queen then he ends up a piece down after 51...♘xe6 52 ♘xe6+ followed by 53 ♘xc5. However, declining the queen is little help as all White's pieces are ready to bear down on Black's exposed king; indeed there is no defence to the immediate threats of 52 ♖d7+ and 52 ♕f7+. The game ended quickly after 51...♖f4 52 ♖d7+ ♔h6 53 ♘f7+ ♔g7 54 ♘e5+ ♔h6 55 ♖xh7+ 1-0 (55...♔xh7 56 ♕f7+ mates next move).

41)

Radjabov – Adams

Rapidplay game, Prague 2002

Black used the potential knight fork on f3 to win the key e4-pawn. The game continued 31...♗xe4! 32 ♕f2 (after 32 ♗xe4 ♕xe4 33 ♖xe4 ♘f3+ 34 ♔f2 ♘xd2 White's rooks are forked and he ends up a whole rook down, so he is forced to decline the sacrifice) 32...♗c6 (the loss of the e4-pawn has wrecked White's position, since Black can now attack along the long light diagonal) 33 h4 ♘f3+ 34 ♖xf3 (34 ♔f1 e4 35 ♗c2 ♖xb2 is also hopeless for White) 34...♗xf3 35 hxg5 fxg5 36 ♕e3 e4 37 ♗f1 ♕e7 38 b4 ♕e5 39 b5 ♕g3+ 0-1. It is mate next move.

42)

Loskutov – Chuprikov

Russian Team Ch, Smolensk 2000

White scored a quick knock-out by 19 ♕d8+ ♔g7 20 ♕xh8+! and Black resigned, because after 20...♔xh8 21 ♘xf7+ followed by ♘xd6 White is a whole rook up.

43)

Sturua – del Rio

Linares open 2001

The fork doesn't exactly leap to the eye but White spotted it nonetheless: 22 ♘xe6! fxe6 (after 22...♕xg3 23 fxg3 ♖fe8 Black's losses are restricted to one pawn, but 24 ♘g5 ♖e7 25 e5 should be winning for White thanks to the pressure against the weak f7-pawn) 23 ♕xg6 hxg6 24 ♗xe6+ ♔h7 25 ♗xd7 ♖xc1 26 ♖xc1 ♖d8? (26...♗xe4 is better, but after 27 f3 ♗d5 28 ♔f2 ♖d8 29 ♖c7 White is a pawn up with a good position and should win) 27 ♖c7 ♗xe4 28 ♖xa7 ♗f5 29 ♗xf5 gxf5 30 a5! bxa5 31 ♖xa5 (White is two clear pawns up and won without difficulty) 31...♔g6 32 ♖a4 f4 33 ♔f1 ♔f5 34 ♔e2 ♖b8 35 ♖a2 ♔e4 36 ♖d2 ♖d8 37 d5 ♖d6 38 ♖d1 ♔f5 39 ♔f3 ♔e5 40 ♖d2 ♔f5 41 ♖d4 1-0.

44)

Koksch – C. Meissner

Germany (Oberliga East) 2000/1

Black should have played 11...f6, and after 12 ♗c4 fxg5 13 0-0 an unclear position arises in which White has a lead in development in return for Black's two extra pawns. However, she instead played 11...h6? and was shocked by the reply 12 ♕d8+! ♔xd8 13 ♘xf7+ ♔c7 14 ♘xe5 leaving White a piece up for just one pawn. The game finished 14...♗f5 15 ♗d3 e6 16 0-0-0 1-0.

45)

Ljubojević – Avrukh

Lost Boys, Amsterdam 1999

The fork is fairly well disguised in this position, but the undefended bishop on e7 is a clue. Play continued **26...c3 27 bxc3** (if White doesn't take this pawn, then it advances to the seventh rank; for example, 27 ♕d3 c2 28 ♖a1 ♗xb2 forking the rooks) **27...♖xb1 28 ♖xb1 ♕e4** (here's the fork; White must lose a piece) **29 ♖b6 ♕xe7 30 ♖xd6 ♗xc3** and Black's material advantage of a piece for two pawns proved sufficient for a win.

46)

Grishchuk – Timman
Wijk aan Zee 2002

White won by **26 g6+!** (the first sacrifice) **26...♗xg6** (after 26...♔f8 27 ♘e6+ ♗xe6 28 ♖xe6 White wins because Black is effectively playing a rook down; a typical line is 28...c5 29 ♖xa6 ♔e7 30 ♗xg7 ♖g8 31 ♗c3 and White is two clear pawns up) **27 ♖e7+!** (the second sacrifice sets the stage for a deadly knight fork) **27...♔xe7 28 ♘xg6+** (White ends up winning a piece for a pawn) **28...♔e6 29 ♘xh8 g5** (Black makes a futile attempt to trap White's knight and when that fails he resigns) **30 ♘g6 c5 31 ♗g7 ♔f5** (31...♔f7 is met by 32 ♘e5+) **32 ♘e7+ ♔e6 33 ♘c6 d4 34 ♔d2 a4 35 c3 ♔d5 36 ♘d8 1-0**.

Solutions to Discovered Attack Exercises

1)

Cicak – Palsson
VISA Grand Prix, Reykjavik 1998

After **30 ♘xd6+** Black resigned, as White follows up with 31 ♖xb7, winning a whole rook.

2)

Morozevich – Galliamova
Russian Ch, St Petersburg 1998

White unveiled a discovered attack on f7 by playing **40 ♗xc5+**. This leads to a quick mate whatever Black plays; for example, 40...♔e8 41 ♕xf7+ ♔d8 42 ♕e7+ ♔c8 43

♖f8#. The game actually ended **40...♘xc5 41 ♕xf7#**.

3)

Xie Jianjun – Landa
Beijing 1997

It certainly wasn't a good idea. After **41...♕xb3?? 42 ♘f5+ exf5 43 ♕xb3** Black resigned, as the discovered attack has cost him his queen.

4)

L. Johannessen – Åkesson
Åsker 1997

No. Instead of moving his rook, Black played **22...d4**, attacking both the queen and the bishop. White must lose a piece, so he resigned.

5)

A. Horvath – Hoang Thanh Trang
Budapest 2002

White won Black's queen by **26 ♗g6+ ♖xg6 27 ♕xa3**, whereupon Black at once resigned.

6)

P. Nikolić – Topalov
Linares 1997

If the knight on g4 were not there, Black could play ...♕xh3#. This provides the motivation for the winning move **22...♘e5**, both attacking the queen and threatening mate in one. White cannot save his queen, so he resigned.

7)

Ibragimov – Schekachev
Russian Ch (rapid playoff), Moscow 1999

No, it wasn't a good idea. Black was so concerned with his own combination that he forgot about his opponent's tactical possibilities. After **14...♖xc3 15 ♖xc3 ♘xe4** White won Black's queen by **16 ♖c8+ ♗xc8 17 ♕xa5** and after **17...♘xg5 18 b6** Black resigned.

8)

Sakaev – Volkov

*FIDE Knockout (rapid playoff),
New Delhi 2000*

Black won the exchange by **18...♗f3**, attacking White's queen and the g1-rook. After **19 ♕xf3 ♖xg1+ 20 ♗f1 ♖d8 21 ♖xd8+ ♔xd8 22 ♕a8+ ♔e7** Black had a decisive material advantage and went on to win.

9)

Weiss – Socko

European Ch, Ohrid 2001

As so often happens, an undefended piece provides the clue hinting that a discovered attack might be possible. After **38 ♗h6!**, the queens face each other, but Black has no time to capture as White is also threatening mate by ♗g7#. Black resigned as he must lose his queen.

10)

Landenbergue – M. Röder

Berne 1993

White played **11 ♘d5!**, discovering an attack on Black's queen. If he replies 11...♕xd2, then 12 ♘c7# is mate. In fact, Black cannot save his queen without allowing the mate on c7, so he resigned. Note that 11 ♘b5 is less effective, as Black can defend by 11...♕b6.

11)

B. Lalić – Kotsur

World Team Ch, Lucerne 1997

Black set up a discovered attack by the rook sacrifice **40...♖xh2+**. White resigned in view of the continuation 41 ♔xh2 ♗xf4+ followed by 42...♕xe2, winning his queen. Note that the simple 40...♕xf4 is ineffective, as White can reply 41 ♕xh5.

12)

Sakaev – Shipov

Russia Cup, St Petersburg 1997

The line-up of the white queen and its undefended black counterpart on h5 suggests a possible discovered attack. White played **28 ♘xe6**, clearing his knight out of the way with gain of tempo. If Black plays 28...fxe6, then he loses his queen to 29 ♖xg7+, while if he moves the queen then White can take on d8. In either case Black faces catastrophic material loss, so he resigned.

13)

Kriventsov – Gulko

USA Ch, Seattle 2002

Play continued **34...♖xc5! 35 ♖e1** (the key line is 35 ♕xc5 ♘c3+ winning the queen) **35...♖xc2 36 ♖xc2 ♗xc2+ 37 ♔a1 ♘xf4**, when Black had a decisive material advantage. The game finished **38 ♖e8+ ♔h7 39 ♕d8 ♘xh5 40 ♖h8+ ♔g6 41 ♕e8+ ♔g5 42 ♕e7+ ♔g4 43 ♖f8 ♕e4 44 ♕d7+ ♔g3 45 ♖e8 f2 0-1**.

14)

Van Wely – Shirov

Ter Apel 1997

The discovered attack isn't especially obvious in the diagram, but it only takes one move to set it up. The exchange **31...♗xf3 32 ♗xf3** both removes the defender of the d4-rook and helps to clear the line g4-d4; now the stage is set for a discovered attack. The game continued **32...♘h3+ 33 ♔g2 ♕xd4 34 ♔xh3 ♗xe5** with a decisive material advantage for Black. The finish was **35 ♘c4 ♗c7 36 ♔g2 ♕d3 37 ♕c1 h5 38 ♘e3 ♗e5 39 ♘c4 ♕c3 40 ♕xc3 ♗xc3 41 ♘d6 ♖d7 42 b5 ♔f8 0-1**.

15)

Svensk – Svidler

Gausdal 1992

The key idea is that of pin-breaking. The f6-knight is apparently pinned, but in fact the knight can move so as to set up a compensating attack on White's queen. The game continued **12...♘xe4! 13 ♘xe4** (13 ♗xd8 ♘xd2 14 ♔xd2 ♖xd8 also leaves Black a pawn up) **13...♕xh4 14 c3** (14 ♘xd6 ♗xb2

15 ♖b1 ♗d4 and again Black has an extra pawn).

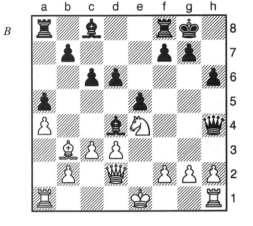

Now Black won by **14...d5!** (the clearest) **15 cxd4 dxe4 16 dxe5 e3! 17 ♕c2** (17 ♕xe3 ♕b4+ wins the bishop) **17...exf2+ 18 ♔f1 ♗e6 19 ♖a3 ♕f4 20 h4 ♖ad8 0-1**.

16)
Burmakin – Kharlov
Russia Cup, Kazan 2001

Black won a pawn with the effective combination **28...♗xa4!**, based on the point 29 ♖xa4 ♘c5 with a discovered attack against the d4-knight. White therefore decided to play **29 ♗b5 e5 30 ♗xa4 exd4 31 ♖ee1**, but Black is a pawn up with a good position. The conclusion was **31...♘c5 32 ♗c6 ♖ac8 33 ♗d5 ♘d3 34 ♖eb1 ♖c5 35 b3 h5 36 ♔g1 ♘f4 37 ♗c4 h4 38 ♖a2 d3 39 ♔f1 ♘e2 40 ♖d2 a4 41 ♖xd3 ♖xd3 42 ♗xd3 ♘f4 43 ♗c4 a3 44 ♖a1 ♖g5 45 ♖d1 ♖xg2 46 ♖d8+ ♔h7 47 ♗xf7 a2 0-1**.

17)
Ahmatović – Medvescek
Slovenian Under-16 Girls Ch, Maribor 2001

White won material with a pin-breaking motif combined with a discovered check: **9 ♘xe5! ♗xd1** (9...♘xe5 10 ♖xe5+ ♗e6 11

♗xd5 also costs Black a piece) **10 ♘xc6+** and Black resigned since White follows up with 11 ♘xd8 and 12 ♖xd1, ending up with an extra piece. This type of tactic occurs relatively often in the opening phase.

18)
San Segundo – Van den Doel
Zonal tournament, Mondariz 2000

There is no discovered check visible in the diagram, but Black can set one up with a few forcing preparatory moves: **22...♗h2+** (White actually resigned here) 23 ♔h1 ♖xe3 (deflecting the f2-pawn) 24 fxe3 (or else White remains a piece down) 24...♘g3+ 25 ♔xh2 (the preparations are over and now the discovered check comes with devastating effect) 25...♘xf1++ followed by 26...♘xd2 and White loses his queen for just one minor piece.

19)
Fedorov – Adianto
Olympiad, Istanbul 2000

Black won by **33...♘ed2+ 34 ♔c1** (34 ♔a2 and 34 ♔a1 are both met by 34...♕a5#) **34...♘b3+!** and White resigned, as 35 cxb3 ♘e3+ (the discovered check), 35 ♔d1 ♘e3+ (a fork) and 35 ♔b1 ♘cd2+ all cost White his queen, in the last case because playing 36 ♔a2 would again allow 36...♕a5#.

20)
Kengis – Hertneck
Bundesliga 1999/00

White played **19 ♘g5!**, discovering an attack against the undefended bishop on b7 and threatening mate on h7. The continuation was **19...♗xg5 20 ♗xg5 ♕xg5 21 ♗xb7 ♖b8** (Black must move the rook, or else he loses the exchange, but now the c7-pawn falls) **22 ♖xc7** and White could be satisfied with the outcome of his combination. He has an extra pawn, and his rook occupies an active position on the seventh rank. The conclusion was **22...♘d5 23 ♗xd5 ♕xd5 24 b3** axb3 25 axb3 e5 26 dxe5 ♕xe5 27 ♕c4 ♖b6 28 ♖d1 ♖f6 29 ♖c8 ♕e7 30 ♕c7 ♕xc7 31 ♖xc7 g6 32 ♖b7 ♖e8 33 e3 and Black resigned, since after 33...♖e4 34 ♖d8+ ♔g7 35 ♖db8 he loses a second pawn, when White's material advantage is decisive.

21)

P. Fröhlich – Motylev
Linares open 2001

The undefended b2-bishop gave Black the chance to win a pawn by **13...♘xe4! 14 ♗xg7** (14 ♘xe4 ♗xb2 also costs White a pawn) **14...♘xd2 15 ♕xd2** (if White retreats the bishop from g7, then Black can win the exchange by taking on f1) **15...♔xg7**. White struggled on for a long time but could not save the game. This type of discovered attack along a long diagonal is quite common in practice.

22)

Salmensuu – Mäki
Finnish Ch, Vammala 1999

The line-up of queen on d2 and undefended queen on a5 is suggestive, and sure enough a discovered attack nets White a pawn: **15 ♘d5! ♕xd2 16 ♘xe7+** (this and the following are **in-between moves** which enable White to seize a pawn before recapturing the queen) **16...♔f8 17 ♗xg7+** (necessary, as the immediate 17 ♖xd2 would lose a piece after 17...♗xd4) **17...♔xe7** (17...♔xg7 18 ♖xd2 also leaves White a pawn up) **18 ♖xd2 ♗xb3 19 axb3 f6** (White is a pawn up, so Black tries to trap the g7-bishop) **20 ♗h6 g5 21 h4** (this frees the bishop and gives White a winning position) **21...♖g8 22 hxg5 fxg5 23 f4 1-0**. Black resigned as White will inevitably win another pawn.

23)

Ma. Tseitlin – Titz
European Clubs Cup, Kallithea 2002

White played **40 ♕xc4!** and Black resigned in view of 40...dxc4 41 ♖d7+ (White sets up a discovered attack along the seventh

rank with gain of tempo) 41...♔a8 (41...♔b8 42 ♗d6+ is one move quicker) 42 ♗xe4+ ♔b8 43 ♗d6+ and White wins the queen, ending up with an extra piece.

24)

Khalifman – Burmakin
Russian Team Ch, St Petersburg 1999

White won quickly by **28 ♖xb7!**, setting up a discovered attack along the h1-a8 diagonal. If 28...♕xb7, then 29 ♘d6+ ♗xd6 30 ♕xb7 wins Black's queen, while 28...♖c8 fails to 29 ♘f6+ ♗xf6 (or 29...gxf6 30 ♕xc6+ ♖xc6 31 ♖b8+ ♗d8 32 ♖bxd8+ ♔e7 33 ♖1d7#) 30 exf6! (threatening mate on e7) 30...gxf6 31 ♖d8+! (a neat finish) 31...♔xd8 32 ♕xf6+ ♔e8 33 ♕e7#. The game actually concluded **28...♖d8 29 ♘f6+** and Black resigned, as White mates in two more moves.

25)

Anand – Lautier
Biel 1997

The two queens are facing each other and Black's queen is undefended, but there is no obvious discovered attack by moving the d3-bishop. However, Anand found a brilliant solution: **21 ♗g6!!**.

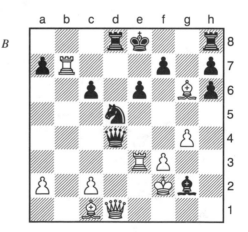

21...♘e7 (Black cannot take the queen because 21...♕xd1 is met by 22 ♖xe6+ ♘e7 23

♖exe7+ ♔f8 24 ♗xh6+ ♔g8 25 ♗xf7#, so he has to retreat the knight, but now that the e3-rook is not under attack White can round up the g2-bishop) **22 ♕xd4 ♖xd4 23 ♖d3** (23 ♗h5 and 23 ♖xe6 are also very strong) **23...♖d8** (after 23...♖xd3 24 ♗xd3, threatening both 25 ♔xg2 and 25 ♖b8+, White wins material) **24 ♖xd8+ ♔xd8 25 ♗d3 1-0**. Black resigned because 25...♗h3 26 ♔g3 and 25...♗h1 26 ♗d2 followed by 27 ♖b1 win the bishop, leaving White a piece up. Note that 21 ♖xf7, hoping for 21...♔xf7 22 ♗g6+, is less effective since Black can reply 21...♕a1! with an unclear position.

26)
Miranda – Tiviakov
New York 1998

It was a very good move. **26...♕xf7** looks like a blunder because it allows White a discovered attack by **27 ♗xe5+ ♔a8** (White actually resigned here) 28 ♕xf7, but it is Black who strikes the final blow by 28...♖xg2+ 29 ♔h1 ♖xf2+ (this discovered check forces mate; 29...♖g7+ is also decisive) 30 ♔g1 ♖g2+ 31 ♔h1 ♖g7+ 32 ♕f3 ♗xf3+ 33 ♖xf3 ♖d1+ 34 ♖f1 ♖xf1#.

Solutions to Pin Exercises

1)
Ibrahim – Russell
Olympiad, Bled 2002

White's d4-pawn is pinned against the undefended queen on d3, so its defence of the c5-bishop is an illusion. Black exploited this by **19...♕xc5**, picking up a piece for nothing. White resigned in due course.

2)
J.C. Hernandez – Millan Urrutia
Linares open 2000

White's e3-rook is pinned against his king and so has no influence horizontally. After **23...♕xd3** White resigned, since he cannot regain the lost piece. Note that the attempt to win Black's queen by 24 ♖xe8+ followed by 25 ♕xd3 fails as the recapture 24...♖xe8+ is check.

3)
Kopionkin – Arkhipov
Russian Team Ch, Smolensk 2000

At the moment the d5-knight is not seriously pinned, because the d8-rook is defended and so moving the knight would cost at most the b7-pawn. However, by **29 ♕b5** White set up a deadly horizontal pin of the knight. The knight is attacked three times but only defended twice, and Black is unable to defend it again. If Black plays 29...a6, then White wins a piece in any case by 30 ♖xd5. The game actually concluded **29...♗c7 30 ♖xd5** and Black resigned, since 30...♕h2+ 31 ♔f1 ♕h1+ 32 ♔e2 is the end of Black's checks, leaving him a piece down.

4)
Mateo – Gongora
Santa Clara 2000

Black played **38...♖d2** and White resigned since the d-file pin costs White a piece.

5)
Czebe – Rajlich
Budapest 2002

White's queen is pinning two black units, the rook on f7 and the pawn on c6. White played **26 ♗d5!**, exploiting both pins with one deadly blow. Black resigned rather than continue 26...♕c7 27 ♕xf7+ ♕xf7 28 ♗xf7+ ♔xf7, when he is the exchange down for nothing and must lose in the end.

6)
Crouch – Eames
British League (4NCL) 2001/2

The b3-rook is pinned horizontally, so is not really defending the other rook. Black resigned after **29 ♕xb8+**, since 29...♖xb8 30 ♖xa3 leaves White a rook up.

7)

Prié – Santo-Roman
French Ch, Narbonne 1997

After **38 c4** Black resigned, as the d5-bishop is pinned along the d-file and so Black must lose a piece.

8)

D. Atlas – Burović
Zonal tournament, Dresden 1998

It is sometimes quite hard to see an impending pin and here White's last move (34 ♗a7-e3) allowed the reply **34...♕e2**.

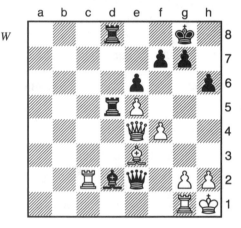

White resigned as the e3-bishop is pinned and doubly attacked; it cannot be defended and so White must lose either a piece or the exchange (after 35 ♖xd2 ♖xd2). In either case his position is hopeless.

9)

Kotsur – Moradiabadi
Asian Ch, Calcutta 2001

It is quite easy to make the false assumption that a piece in the middle of one's own position must be defended. White evidently failed to notice that his rook on f1 was unprotected and therefore the e2-rook was pinned. Black played **30...♘xc2! 31 ♕c1 ♘d4** winning a vital pawn, which he eventually converted into victory.

10)

Hraček – Oll
Polanica Zdroj 1996

The pin along the fourth rank proved fatal after **20 ♗g5+ ♔g7 21 ♗e7+**.

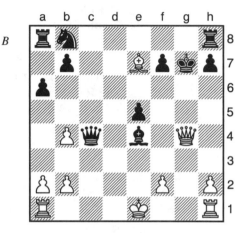

Black resigned because 21...♔h6 22 ♕g5# is mate, while 21...♗g6 allows White to win Black's queen.

11)

Nguyen Anh Dung – Maiwald
Budapest 1999

The pin along the line c1-e3 neutralizes the rook on d2, opening up the possibility of capturing on g2. Nevertheless Black has to take care, because 36...♖xg2+? loses to 37 ♖xg2 ♕xe3 38 ♖dxg7+ ♔h8 39 ♖g8+ ♔h7 40 ♖2g7#. This variation illustrates the necessity of following each line through to the end so as not to overlook tactical possibilities for the opponent. The correct solution is **36...♗xg2!**, when White resigned as he has no real defence to the threat of 37...♕h1#.

12)

Kovačević – Hulak
Croatian Ch, Pula 2000

The g2-pawn is pinned against a possible ...♕g1#, so Black was able to play **46...♖f3!** secure in the knowledge that the rook is immune to capture by the g2-pawn. Rather surprisingly, the white queen is trapped and heavy material loss is inevitable. The game ended **47 g3 ♕b2** (Black has several ways to win, but after trapping the enemy queen he couldn't resist offering his own) **48 ♖g2** (after 48 ♖xb2 axb2 Black wins White's queen and creates a new one of his own on b1) **48...♖xf4 49 ♖xf4 ♕c3** (White is too far behind on material) **50 ♘f1 c6 51 dxc6+ ♔xc6 52 ♖e2 ♖d6 53 ♖ff2 ♖d3 54 ♖c2 ♕d4 55 ♖ce2 ♔d6 56 ♖f4 ♔c7 57 h4 ♖f3 58 ♖xf3 exf3 59 ♖d2 ♕e5 60 ♔g1 0-1**.

13)

Dydyshko – Navara

European Team Ch, Leon 2001

It was tempting to grab the rook on c8, but this move proved a fatal mistake. The d3-pawn is pinned and so cannot effectively defend the e4-pawn. Black exploited this by **23...♗xe4!**, threatening mate on both g2 and h1.

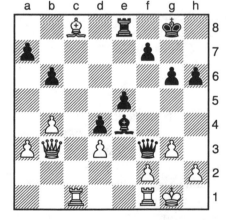

White can only avoid mate by giving up his queen, and the game concluded **24 ♕xf7+** (24 dxe4 ♕xb3 is also hopeless for White) **24...♔xf7 25 dxe4 ♕xe4 26 ♗a6 ♕f3 27 ♖fd1 ♕xa3 28 ♗d3 e4 29 ♗c4+ ♔f6 30 ♖a1 ♕xb4 31 ♖xd4 ♖c8 32 ♖ad1 ♖xc4 33 ♖d6+ ♔e7 0-1**.

14)

Machulsky – Pavlović

Belgrade-Moscow match 1998

No, Black cannot win a pawn. He believed he could grab one by **28...♖xd4?** (Black should have played 28...♖h8 instead), exploiting the pins along the lines c8-c1 and g5-c1. However, Black overlooked **29 f4!** breaking the g5-c1 pin with gain of tempo.

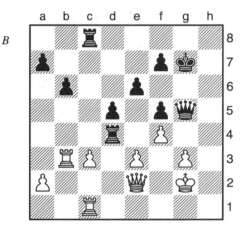

Now Black's queen and d4-rook are both under attack, and heavy material loss is inevitable. The game ended **29...♕h6 30 ♖h1 ♕xh1+ 31 ♔xh1 ♖dc4 32 ♔g2 ♔f6 33 ♕d2 ♔e7 34 ♔f3 1-0**.

15)

Lautier – Bologan

Enghien-les-Bains 1999

White won by **9 ♕a4+ ♗d7** (9...b5 loses material after 10 ♗xb5+ axb5 11 ♕xa8) **10 ♘xd7** and Black resigned as after 10...♕xd7 11 ♗b5 (again utilizing the pin along the a-file) 11...axb5 12 ♕xa8+ ♕d8 13 ♕xb7 White wins the exchange and a pawn.

16)

Stangl – Lehner

Mitropa Cup, Baden 1999

First of all one must note the two pins already in existence, along the lines c6-h1 and e8-e1. The first pin means that the d5-knight isn't defending the e3-bishop, which is itself limited in mobility because of the second pin. Black played **31...♗h6**, stepping up the pressure on the pinned bishop, which is now attacked three times and only defended twice. White cannot defend the e3-bishop again, so loss of material is inevitable. Following **32 ♔g1** (unpinning the d5-knight and so providing a temporary extra defence of e3, but Black can easily eliminate this defender) **32...♗xd5** White resigned since after 33 ♕xd5 (33 cxd5 ♗xe3+ also wins for Black) 33...♕xd5 34 cxd5 ♖xe3 Black wins a piece.

17)

Estrada Nieto – Szeberenyi
Budapest 2001

Although there are three pieces between the c1-rook and Black's queen, White won material with a typical combination. **14 ♘d5! exd5** (Black has little choice; 14...♕b8 and 14...♕c8 lose to 15 ♘xc6 bxc6 16 ♘xe7+, while 14...♕d7 15 ♘b6 forks queen and rook, winning the exchange) **15 cxd5** (now the c6-knight is pinned and attacked three times; Black cannot reasonably defend it, and so White wins a pawn) **15...♘d7 16 dxc6 bxc6 17 ♖xc6**. White is a pawn up with a large positional advantage, and won in a few moves.

18)

Lutz – Bangiev
German Ch, Bremen 1998

The f6-knight is already pinned against the black queen. White added a second pin by **20 ♗g4**, immobilizing the other knight. Black's position depends on the knights being able to defend each other, so it is not surprising that it now collapses. The immediate threat is to take the f6-knight, which is now attacked twice and defended only once. If Black plays 20...♔c7, then 21 ♗xd7 ♖xd7 22 ♖xd7+ wins material, while 20...♘g8 21 ♕xe7 ♘xe7 22 ♘xf7 ♖de8 23 ♘d6+ is also disastrous. Black therefore resigned.

19)

Alonso – Gomez Baillo
Argentine Ch, Buenos Aires 1998

In the diagram Black's rook and knight are attacked, and he also faces a possible discovered check if White moves his bishop. However, Black was able to resolve these difficulties and even win a piece: **33...♕e4+!** (clearing the way for the c3-rook to retreat to c7) **34 ♔a1 ♖c7** (now the bishop is pinned and White must lose a piece) **35 ♕xd5+** (White grabs a second pawn for the piece, but the endgame is hopeless) **35...♕xd5 36 ♖xd5 ♖xe7 37 f4 ♔c6 38 ♖d8 ♔c5 39 ♔b1 ♘d4 40 ♖f8 ♔d5 41 f5 ♔xe5 42 f6 ♖d7 0-1**.

20)

Rogić – Morrison
European Ch, Ohrid 2001

There is no obvious pin in the diagram, but White was able to set one up with two preliminary captures: **24 ♘xe6 fxe6 25 ♖xe6!** (this forces a decisive material gain) **25...♕d7** (the key line is 25...♕xe6 26 ♗d5, pinning and winning Black's queen; in the game Black avoids this fate, but ends up a piece down) **26 ♗xd5 ♔h8 27 ♗xc4 ♕xd1+ 28 ♖xd1 ♗xf4 29 gxf4 ♖ac8 30 ♖d4 b5 31 ♗f1 ♖xc3 32 ♖xa6 1-0**.

21)

Morozevich – Adams
Wijk aan Zee 2001

The preliminary exchange **26...♗xc3 27 ♕xc3** drew White's queen onto the third rank and so pinned the g3-pawn horizontally. Then came the deadly blow **27...♘h4!** and White resigned since Black threatens mate on g2; preventing it will cost White his queen.

22)

Anoori – Ravi
Calcutta 2001

A preliminary sacrifice set White up for a decisive pin: **39...♖xd4! 40 ♖xd4 ♗c5 41**

♔e3 b3 (Black decides to promote his b-pawn; 41...♔xe5 winning the rook is just as good) **42 ♔d3 ♗xd4 43 ♔xd4 b2 44 ♔e4 b1♕+** with an easy win.

23)

Nolte – Yurtaev
Asian Ch, Calcutta 2001

The game continued **25...♖xg3+ 26 ♕xg3** (or 26 hxg3 ♕h1#) **26...♖g8** (now that the white queen has been drawn onto the g-file, Black is able to pin it) **27 ♖e8** (this sideways pin is the only way to avoid loss of the queen, but White ends up a piece down in any case) **27...♕xg3+ 28 hxg3 ♖xe8 29 ♔f2 ♗g4 30 ♖e1 ♖e4 31 ♖e3 ♔g7 0-1**.

24)

Sofronie – Manea
Team event, Eforie Nord 2000

The g2-bishop is pinned horizontally, and this gave Black the option to invade with his queen by **20...♕h3!**. White resigned as material loss is inevitable. Black's principal threat is 21...♕xg3 followed by ...♖h1#; the two main defences are 21 ♗xh3 ♖xe2, which wins a piece because both white bishops are under attack, and 21 ♗f4 ♖h1+ 22 ♗xh1 (22 ♔f2 ♕xg2+! 23 ♔xg2 ♖8h2#) 22...♕xh1+ 23 ♔f2 ♖h2+, which wins the white queen with check.

25)

Seul – Miezis
Bad Godesburg 1996

Yes, he does. Black won by **35...♕h2+ 36 ♔f1 ♖f8+ 37 ♗f3** (or 37 ♕f3 ♖xf3+ 38 ♗xf3 ♕f2#) **37...♕h1#**, the final mate making use of the pin along the f-file.

26)

Strenzke – Richter
Hamburg 1999

The d4-bishop is pinned against the possibility of ♕d8+ followed by mate, so **22 ♗c3** proved decisive. The bishop is now also pinned against the queen, so Black cannot play 22...♗b6, and it cannot be defended. Thus the bishop is lost and Black resigned.

27)

Lagowski – Tomczak
Polish Ch, Warsaw 2002

The winning combination is quite hard to see, because at the moment there is no trace of a possible pin. The continuation was **19 ♘xc6! ♘xc6 20 ♘d5!** (White is attacking both b6 and c7, so if the queen moves then White regains his piece with an extra pawn) **20...♘xd5** (20...♗xd5 21 cxd5 wins a pawn in the same way) **21 cxd5** (now the pin materializes; White has a triple attack against the pinned c6-knight) **21...♗f7** (the attempt to regain the lost pawn by 21...♗d7 22 dxc6 ♖ac8? fails to 23 ♕a2+) **22 dxc6** (not only has White won a pawn, but the powerful c6-pawn gives him a large positional advantage) **22...♖fb8 23 ♖b7 ♖a2** (after 23...♖xb7 24 cxb7 ♕xc2 25 bxa8♕+ White wins a rook) **24 ♕b1 ♖xb7 25 cxb7** and Black resigned, since 25...♕b8 26 ♖c1 followed by ♖c8+ is decisive.

28)

Romanishin – Beliavsky
Lvov 2000

At first sight White cannot take on a6 because the pawn appears to be pinned against the undefended rook on b2. However, White played **22 bxa6!** based on the counter-pin 22...♖xb2 23 ♕a1 and Black loses the rook on b2, with the net result that White has won an important pawn on a6. Black therefore preferred **22...♖a8**, trying to regain the pawn on a6. However, while Black is achieving this, White has time to gain a decisive advantage in other areas. The game ended **23 ♕d3 ♘e5 24 ♕c3** (threatening gxf4, winning the pinned knight) **24...♘g7 25 ♖fb1 ♖xa6 26 gxf4 ♘d7** (26...♖xf4 runs into yet another pin after 27 ♖b8) **27 ♘g5** (Black is not only a pawn down but his position is wrecked)

27...&g8 28 ②e6 ♕f6 29 ♕xc7 ②xe6 30 dxe6 ♕xe6 31 ♖b7 ♖f7 32 ♕c8+ ②f8 33 ♕xe6 ②xe6 34 ♗d5 1-0.

29)
Acs – Korchnoi
European Ch, Ohrid 2001

It certainly wasn't a good idea. Black intended to reach a rook and pawn ending with an extra pawn, but the counter-pin **33 ♖a8!** turned the tables completely.

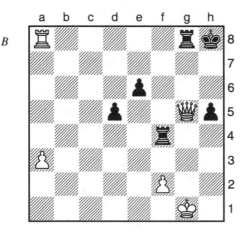

Black's only hope is to play 33...♖g4+, but after 34 ♕xg4 hxg4 35 ♖xg8+ &xg8 36 a4 Black is unable to stop White's a-pawn, while White's king easily copes with Black's nearby d-pawn. Therefore Black resigned. This is a further example of a player initiating tactics but overlooking a tactical possibility for his opponent.

30)
Jonkman – Firman
Lvov 2001

There is no obvious pin in the diagram but a series of forcing moves set one up along the a7-g1 diagonal: **27...♖xc1** (this preliminary exchange permits a later ...②b3) **28 ♕xc1 ♗xb5** (28...②b3 is also effective; it doesn't matter if Black inverts this move and his next) **29 ♗xb5** (29 axb5 is met the same way)

and here White resigned without waiting for 29...②b3 30 ♕b2 ②xd4 31 ♕xd4 (or else White remains a piece down) 31...♗c5 pinning the queen.

31)
Glek – Hernando Rodrigo
European Clubs Cup, Kallithea 2002

White should have played 28 ♖e5 with a roughly equal position, but instead he chose the tactical **28 ②xe6? fxe6 29 ♖e5** relying on the e-file pin to escape from the double attack of Black's e6-pawn. However, Black spotted the error in White's idea and replied **29...♕xc5!**. This move wins a rook, because 30 ♖xc5 can be met by 30...exf5 when Black has an extra piece in the ending. The game in fact concluded **30 ♕f4 ♕xc2 31 ♖e4 ②d5 0-1**.

Solutions to Skewer Exercises

1)
Chabanon – Relange
French Ch, Méribel 1998

Black's queen and bishop are lined up ready for a skewer. After **40 ♖d5** Black has to move his queen, for example by 40...♕b4, when White can win a piece by 41 ♕xd7 (41 ♖xd7 also wins). Then Black has no time to take on c4, because his own e8-rook is attacked. He therefore resigned.

2)
Bareev – Fedorov
FIDE World Cup, Shenyang 2000

White continued **39 ♕b8+** when Black must move his king. However, this leaves his bishop undefended and after **39...&d7 40 ♕xe5** Black resigned since White is a pawn up with two connected passed pawns and in addition Black's king is hopelessly exposed.

3)

Wells – Arlandi

Zonal tournament, Escaldes 1998

White's queen has ventured into enemy territory and now suffers thanks to a line-up with the a3-knight. After **18...♖a8** Black wins, since 19 ♗xa8 ♖xa8 20 ♕b7 ♖xa3 wins bishop and knight for rook. Black would also have a large positional advantage (light-squared control and weak white pawns) so White decided to resign immediately.

4)

Loginov – Nevostruev

Russian Team Ch, St Petersburg 1999

Black won a piece by **35...♖xe3! 0-1**. After 36 ♔xe3 ♗h6+ Black picks up the c1-rook with a skewer.

5)

Yermolinsky – Seirawan

Merrillville 1997

No, **36...g6?** wasn't a good move because it allowed White to win a rook by **37 ♖h8**.

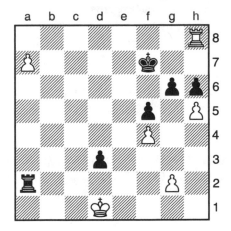

This threatens to promote the pawn, but if Black plays 37...♖xa7 then the skewer 38 ♖h7+ decides the game; Black therefore resigned. Instead of 36...g6?, Black should have moved his rook along the a-file, when he would have had chances to draw the game.

6)

Van der Weide – I. Sokolov

Dutch Ch, Rotterdam 1998

Black won a rook by **58...♖d4+ 59 ♔f5 ♖h5+** and here White resigned in anticipation of 60 ♔f6 (after 60 ♔e6 ♖d6+ White loses a rook at once) 60...♖d6+ 61 ♖e6 ♖h6+ and an unusual skewer picks up a rook.

Solutions to Deflection Exercises

1)

Jacimović – Trkaljanov

European Ch, Ohrid 2001

The motif is the same as in Bui Vinh-Frey on page 47. Black's rook has the important duty of defending the queen, and when White lobbed in **34 ♖e8+** Black faced loss of material after 34...♖xe8 35 ♕xd6 or 34...♔g7 35 ♖xd8. He therefore resigned. Whether one views this as a deflection or as a fork (of h8 and d8) is largely a matter of taste.

2)

Radulski – Shanava

European Ch, Batumi 2002

Black's f8-rook has the important duty of preventing mate on f7, but White managed to deflect it by **41 ♖g8+**. Black resigned in view of the impending mate by 41...♖xg8 42 ♘f7#.

3)

Mehmeti – Weber

European Team Ch, Leon 2001

White's queen must retain control of b1, or else Black mates there, so **38...♗e5+** wins. White resigned as it is mate in two moves.

4)

Nisipeanu – Soln

Ljubljana 2002

The f8-rook must guard f7, or else White mates in two by ♕xf7+ followed by ♕g7# or

♕h7#. Thus the deflection **34 ♖c8!** forced immediate resignation.

5)
Malishauskas – Asauskas
Lithuanian Ch, Vilnius 2002

I make no apologies for including another example of a theme we have seen before, since its importance is such that plenty of practice is well justified. White played **21 ♖d8+** and Black resigned, as 21...♖xd8 loses to 22 ♕xc5, while 21...♘e8 and 21...♗f8 both cost Black a rook after 22 ♕xc5 ♖xc5 23 ♖xa8.

6)
Kriventsov – Sagalchik
USA Ch, Seattle 2002

Black's h5-knight has two duties, defending f4 and g7. However, because White's attacks on f4 and g7 employ the same piece (his queen) he has to take care to choose the right capture to exploit Black's predicament. The game continued **30 ♗xg7+** (this is the correct capture, since if Black plays 30...♘xg7 he loses his queen) **30...♔h7** (Black must decline the offer, but now he loses too much material) **31 ♗c2+ f5 32 ♕xf4 ♘xf4 33 ♗xf8 ♖xf8 34 ♘xd8 ♖xd8 35 ♗xf5+ ♔h8 36 ♖d4 1-0**.

7)
Saravanan – D. Howell
British Ch, Torquay 2002

After **35 ♕f6+!** Black resigned, since after 35...♕xf6 36 gxf6+ Black loses a rook, no matter whether he retreats his king to the first rank or plays 36...♔xf6.

8)
Van Wely – Grishchuk
Wijk aan Zee 2002

16 h3? wasn't a good move, since White's g2-bishop already has the duty of defending the knight on d5. Therefore Black was able to play **16...♗xh3** with impunity, winning an

important pawn. He went on to win the game using his material advantage.

9)
Bykov – Nikolenko
Russia Cup, Moscow 1999

Black spotted that the f3-knight has the vital duty of preventing mate at h2, and continued **14...♘d2!**.

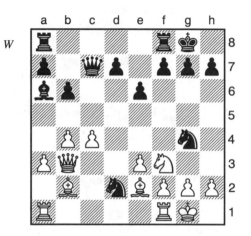

W

White cannot take this knight in view of immediate mate, while if he moves the queen then Black mates in any case by 15...♘xf3+ and 16...♕xh2#. It could be argued that White was lucky not to have to resign immediately, but after **15 ♗e5 ♘xf3+ 16 ♗xf3 ♘xe5 17 ♗xa8 ♗xc4 18 ♖fc1 ♖xa8** it made no difference to the final result as Black had a decisive material superiority. The finish was **19 h3 d5 20 a4 ♕e7 21 ♕c3 ♘d3 22 ♖cb1 ♕h4 23 ♕d2 e5 24 b5 h6 25 a5 ♖e8 26 axb6 axb6 27 f3 e4 28 f4 ♕g3 29 ♖f1 ♗xb5 30 ♖ab1 ♗c4 0-1**.

10)
Zaja – Novak
Croatian Ch, Pula 2000

Black's queen must cover f8, or else White mates by ♕xf8#. The simplest route to victory is **32 ♗h5!**, winning the queen, since it cannot move so as to retain its defence of f8.

11)

Kacheishvili – Fedorowicz
New York 1999

Black spotted that the c3-knight must defend against a possible mate by ...♗xe4#, and after the deflection **48...♘a2!** White was under intolerable pressure. The continuation was **49 ♗e1** (the only way to avoid losing a piece) **49...♘xc3** and White resigned as 50 ♗xc3 ♗xe4+ followed by ...♗xd5 leaves Black with two extra connected passed pawns in the ending.

12)

A. Naiditsch – Brenke
Lippstadt 1999

This winning idea is similar to that of Topalov-Kasparov on page 47. The conclusion was **33...♖xf2+! 34 ♔xf2 ♕h2+** and White resigned in view of 35 ♔f1 ♖f8+ followed by mate next move.

13)

Kiselev – Gubaidullin
Russian Team Ch, St Petersburg 1999

This innocent-seeming position was decided by the deflection of the e1-rook, which has the duty of preventing mate in two by ...♗e4+. Black played **30...♖c1!** and White resigned as he loses at least a rook.

14)

Markidis – Halkias
Greek Ch, Athens 1998

Black's rook must defend against ♖g8#, so White was able to bring his queen into the attack with gain of tempo by **22 ♕xf5!**. Black limped on by **22...♕d8** (22...♖d8 23 ♕f7 mates on g7 or g8), but White's attack, reinforced by the arrival of the queen, proved decisive: **23 ♕g4 ♗g5** (or 23...♕e7 24 ♕g8+ ♖xg8 25 ♖xg8#) **24 ♕xg5** (24 ♗b2! is even better, but of course regaining the sacrificed piece is enough to win) **24...♕xg5 25 ♖xg5** (Black is two pawns down, so he tries to grab one back...) **25...♘xb4** (...but now he runs

into a forced mate) **26 ♗b2** (Black can do little about White's lethal discovered check) **26...♘xd5 27 e6+ 1-0**. It is mate in three more moves; e.g., 27...♘f6 28 e7 ♖f7 29 e8♕+ ♖f8 30 ♕xf8# or 27...♘f6 28 ♖ag1 h6 29 ♖g8+ ♔h7 30 ♖1g7#.

15)

Koziak – Labensky
Rovno 2000

A preliminary sacrifice is necessary to set the stage for the decisive deflection. Black continued **14...♗f2+! 15 ♕xf2** (now the white king has the duty of defending the queen, and so the situation is ripe for a deflection) **15...♖xd1+ 16 ♔e2 ♖a1** (16...♗c4+! 17 bxc4 ♖xe4+ 18 ♗e3 ♕b1 would have been devastating, but the move played proved surprisingly effective) **0-1**. A rather early resignation by White, although after 17 ♕xb6 ♖xa2+ 18 ♔e3 axb6 Black's material advantage should be enough to win in the long run.

16)

Ardeleanu – Vajda
Romanian Ch, Iasi 1999

White can't win with the simple 23 hxg4 since Black would reply 23...♗xg3. Instead White utilized the fact that the f6-knight has to prevent both ♗h7+ and ♖xg4+. The only real question is which of these two moves is effective. 23 ♖xg4+? ♘xg4 24 ♗h7+? ♔h8 is completely wrong since White's queen is under attack and so his discovered checks are ineffective. The correct sequence is **23 ♗h7+ ♘xh7 24 ♖xg4+**, which wins Black's queen. The game ended **24...♕xg4 25 hxg4 ♖e6 26 ♕d2 ♖b8 27 g3** and Black resigned, as White's material advantage is too great.

17)

Kožul – Nisipeanu
European Team Ch, Batumi 1999

Yes. Black could have won the game by 25...♗xc4 26 ♕xc4 ♖d1+, with decisive material gains.

18)

Akhmylovskaya-Donaldson – Wang Pin
USA-China Summit, Shanghai 2002

White's f3-bishop has the task of preventing mate by ...♘g4#. Black exploited this by **42...♕xg2+!** when White resigned as it is mate after 43 ♗xg2 ♘g4#.

19)

Lahner – Vesely
Ostrava 2002

Black's queen is tied to the duty of preventing ♕f6+, so White continued **27 ♖xb7!** (now the black queen cannot retain control of f6) **27...♕xb7 28 ♕f6+** (Black's king is driven out to its doom) **28...♔xh5 29 ♔g2 1-0**. Black cannot meet the threat of 30 ♖h1+ followed by either 31 ♕f3# or 31 f3#.

20)

Motylev – J. Polgar
European Clubs Cup, Kallithea 2002

If White's queen were absent then Black would be able to take both bishop and rook with check, so it is worth sacrificing material to deflect the white queen. After **30...♗f4!** White resigned, as the queen cannot maintain its guard of d3. Note that 30...♗h4 is inferior as White can reply 31 ♕d6.

21)

Vladimirov – Murshed
Asian Ch, Calcutta 2001

Because White is already a piece down, it is no good to win Black's queen by 28 ♖xg7+ ♕xg7 29 ♗xg7 ♖c1+ 30 ♗f1 ♔xg7. Then White's attack would have disappeared, his bishop would be awkwardly pinned and he would have no genuine defence against the deadly threat of ...♗c4. White has to do more than simply win the queen on g7, and the key idea leading to success is a deflection. The game continued **28 ♗xa6! ♕xa6** (28...♕c7 loses to 29 ♗xg7, since 29...♕c1+ 30 ♗f1 gives White a winning attack, or 29...♕xg7 30 ♖xg7+ ♔xg7 31 ♗xc8 with a decisive

material advantage) **29 ♖xg7+** (now White has a forced mate) **29...♔h8 30 ♕f7** and Black resigned, since mate on g8 cannot be prevented.

22)

M. Přibyl – Konopka
Prague 2000

White's queen must defend the c2-rook, while the knight on c5 is preventing mate by ...♖d1+ followed by ...♕d3#. All this means that neither piece is effectively covering a6, a fact which Black exploited by **32...♗a6+!**. The sacrifice cannot be declined, since 33 ♔e1 ♖d1# is mate, while 33 ♔g1 loses to 33...♖d1+ 34 ♔h2 ♕h4#. If White plays 33 ♕xa6, then 33...♖xc2 gives Black a decisive advantage since he is ahead on material and White's king remains very exposed. White chose the only remaining option, **33 ♘xa6**, but after **33...♖d1+** he resigned since it is mate next move by 34 ♔e2 ♕d3#.

23)

Van Wely – Acs
Hoogeveen 2002

Black continued **18...♗g3!**, threatening mate on f2. There is no defence; for example, 19 fxg3 ♗h3#, 19 ♔e2 ♕xf2#, 19 ♖e2 ♕h1# or 19 ♕c2 ♗xd3+ (a deflection) 20 ♕xd3 ♕xf2#. Playing 19 ♘e7+ ♔h8 first doesn't change the situation.

24)

Landa – Ibragimov
Russian Ch, St Petersburg 1998

Black won with the spectacular sacrifice of both his bishops, starting with **22...♗c4!**. The main line runs 23 ♕xc4 (23 ♕d1 loses to 23...♘xe4) 23...♗xf2+! 24 ♔xf2 (after 24 ♔e2 ♕xg3 there is no real defence to the threat of 25...♕f3+) 24...♖xd2+ 25 ♔e3 ♖xc2 and White is not only a pawn down, but his position is completely shattered and his king hopelessly exposed. White therefore resigned straight away.

25)

Zschäbitz – Dworakowska
Barlinek 2001

The game continued **25...♖xc2+! 26 ♕xc2** (26 ♔xc2 allows 26...♕b2#) **26...♖c8!** (this is the deflection) **27 ♔d2** (other moves are even worse; e.g., 27 ♕xc8 ♕b2# or 27 ♖d2 ♕a1#) **27...♖xc2+ 28 ♔xc2 ♕b2+ 29 ♔d3 ♕d4+** (now Black picks up the bishop with a fork, securing a decisive material advantage) **30 ♔e2 ♕xb4 31 ♔f3 ♕c3+ 32 ♔e2 ♕e3+ 0-1**.

26)

Barbeau – Charbonneau
Montreal 2001

If Black's queen were not guarding d7, then White would have a spectacular forced mate by 1 ♘d7+ (1 ♕f6+! and 2 ♘d7+ also works) 1...♔f7 2 ♕f6+! ♖xf6 3 ♘g5#. This suggests that a deflection might be in the air, and White continued with the modest but deadly **43 b3!**.

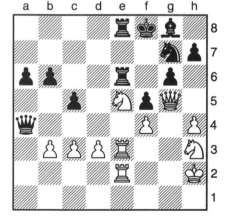

Black cannot maintain his guard on d7 for long, since 43...♕b5 is met by 44 c4, but once ♘d7+ becomes possible White can mate as above. Black therefore tried the desperate **43...h6**, but lost after **44 ♕xh6** (44 ♘xg6+ also wins) **44...♖xe5** (44...♕xb3 45 ♘xg6+ ♔f7 46 ♘g5+ is devastating) **45 bxa4** (45

fxe5 ♕xb3 46 ♘f4 is even better) **45...♖xe3 46 ♖xe3 ♖xe3 47 ♕xg6 1-0**. Black is too much material down.

27)

Pedzich – Murdzia
Swidnica 1999

White found a spectacular win by **25 ♖xd6!** (this deflection forces Black's queen to abandon its defence of the f7-square) **25...♕xd6 26 ♗h7+!** (a second sacrifice, but not a deflection; White just wants to get rid of his bishop with gain of tempo so that his queen can enter the attack) **26...♔xh7** (26...♖xh7 27 ♕f7+ ♔h8 28 ♕e8+ mates next move) **27 ♕g6+ ♔g8 28 ♕f7+** (making use of the preliminary sacrifice on d6) **28...♔h7 29 ♖xh6+!** (a final deflection sacrifice which draws Black's king out for the mate) and Black resigned since 29...♔xh6 30 ♕g6# is mate.

Solutions to Trapped Piece Exercises

1)

Shaked – Kasparov
Tilburg 1997

Black played **20...♗e5** and White resigned since his queen is trapped.

2)

Seminara – Gomez Baillo
Argentine Ch, Buenos Aires 1998

No, he can't get away with **20 ♕xg7**. White probably calculated that after 20...♖g8 21 ♕xh6 his queen could escape, but Black played **20...♖h7** instead, trapping the queen. White therefore resigned.

3)

Holmsten – Minasian
Ubeda 2000

Black trapped White's queen by **23...♘d5**. Although White managed to avoid actually losing his queen, he ended up a piece down after **24 ♘xe5 ♗xe5 25 ♕c6 ♕xc6 26 bxc6**. The finish was **26...♖fc8 27 ♖fe1 f6 28 g3 g5 29 ♖c4 ♖xc6 30 a4 ♖ac8 31 ♗xd4 ♖xc4 32 dxc4 ♗xd4 33 cxd5 ♖c2 0-1**. After 34 ♖f1 White is paralysed and Black can easily start rounding up White's pawns.

4)
Kholmov – Shinkevich
Russia Cup, Perm 1997

White could have won by 27 ♖xe5! ♕xe5 28 ♗f4, trapping Black's queen in mid-board. However, he overlooked this possibility and the game continued **27 ♗a4? ♖e7?** (Black also misses the sacrifice on e5; had he seen it, he surely would have played 27...♗d4+ to remove his bishop from the vulnerable e5-square) **28 ♗c6** (once again, White could have won by 28 ♖xe5, but this time it doesn't matter much, since Black has nothing better than moving his attacked rook) **28...♖b8 29 ♖xe5!** (finally he sees it!) **1-0**.

5)
Kurajica – Sturua
European Team Ch, Pula 1997

After **41 ♘e3** Black resigned, as his rook is captured immediately on every square apart from d2, but 41...♖d2 runs into the knight fork 42 ♘c4+, when the rook is lost in any case.

6)
Seminara – Giaccio
Argentine Ch, Buenos Aires 1998

White's queen is not actually trapped here, but it is so short of squares that Black can secure a decisive material advantage. The game continued **13...g5! 14 ♕xe4** (14 ♕g4 h5 15 ♕h3 g4 is even worse for White, since he loses a piece without gaining any counterplay) **14...♗xe4 15 ♘xe4 h6** and Black has won White's queen for a bishop and a knight. Although White has some counterplay, it is not sufficient and Black won in due course.

7)
Pavasović – Rogulj
Zonal tournament, Dresden 1998

The immediate 17 ♘a4 is met by 17...♕d4, but the preliminary **17 c5!** proved decisive, since 17...dxc5 18 ♘a4 now traps the queen. Black loses at least a piece and so resigned.

8)
Galego – Hauchard
Zonal tournament, Mondariz 2000

It wasn't a good idea as Black trapped the rook using his king: **18...♔d7 19 ♖xc8** (White has no choice, since 19 ♖b6 ♔c7 is even worse for him) **19...♖xc8 20 a3 ♔e6** and Black was material up (rook for knight and pawn) which he eventually exploited to win the game.

9)
Spangenberg – Seminara
Argentine Ch, Buenos Aires 1998

White played **22 g4**, attacking the queen. It has only one safe square to flee to, but after 22...♕e6 23 ♖b6 the queen is trapped and White wins a piece. Black resigned at once.

10)
Saravanan – Thipsay
Guntur 2000

Black's bishop has ventured into enemy territory and after **30 ♘g4**, cutting off the escape-route to h6, it was in serious trouble. The continuation was **30...♖de8 31 ♔f3** and Black faced unavoidable material loss. The game finished **31...♘f7** (31...♖g8 32 ♘xf6 ♖xg3+ 33 ♔xg3 ♘xf5+ 34 ♔g4 ♘h6+ 35 ♔f3 gives White the decisive material advantage of rook and pawn for bishop) **32 ♘xe3 ♘e5+ 33 ♔f2 ♖g8 34 ♖e4 1-0**.

11)
Paramonov – Tarasov
Petroff memorial, St Petersburg 2000

White played **12 axb5**. If Black replies 12...♖xb5, then White wins material with a variety of tactical motifs: 13 ♗a4 (a skewer of rook and knight) 13...♖b6 14 d5 (pin of knight against rook) and Black loses the exchange. In the game Black played **12...axb5**, but after **13 d5** his c6-knight was unexpectedly trapped. The continuation was **13...♗b7 14 dxc6 ♗xc6 15 ♕c2**, and White won with the extra piece.

12)
V. Mikhalevski – Ikonnikov
Vlissingen 1998

White's queen and knight are under threat, but Black's own queen is attacked. White avoided 33 ♖xb6?? which loses the exchange to 33...♕xc1+, and 33 ♕h4? ♕b7, when Black keeps his extra pawn. Instead, he continued **33 ♖xc8 ♘xa4 34 ♖c4!**, trapping the knight. Black resigned at once.

13)
Khurtsidze – Vokarev
Moscow 2002

It doesn't look as if the white queen can be trapped, as it has a3 and c7 available as escape-routes. However, Black revealed the fallacy of this logic by **26...♘c3!**. White resigned, because after the attacked rook moves Black plays ...♘b5, trapping the queen. One cannot emphasize often enough that great caution must be exercised before sending the queen off on a lone journey into the enemy position.

14)
Comas Fabrego – Morović
Capablanca memorial, Havana 1999

White's queen and knight have taken up attacking positions, but without enough support from his other forces. Both pieces are rather short of squares, and the possibility of ...g5 is an ever-present danger. At the moment this can be met by ♕h5, so Black played the subtle **20...♕e8!** taking away the h5-square and threatening to trap White's queen by 21...g5. The only defence to this is

21 ♘g4, which looks a good reply as it threatens both to take on f6 and to play ♕h6+.

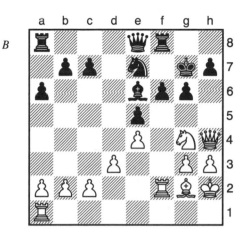

However, the second subtle retreating move **21...♘g8!** proved deadly as it met all White's threats and in addition renewed the threat of ...g5 trapping the queen. There is no real answer to this and, faced by the loss of at least a piece, White resigned.

15)
Pavasović – Beliavsky
Vidmar memorial, Portorož 1999

The rook is a liability. An active rook on the seventh rank is normally an asset, but as always one must take care with pieces that venture into enemy territory. Here White had not been alert to the danger, and after **31...♗e6**, cutting off the rook's retreat, he could not meet the threat of 32...♗d6 33 ♖b7 ♗c8 winning material. The finish was **32 ♗a6 ♗d6 33 ♖b7 ♗c8 34 ♘b2 ♗xb7 35 ♗xb7 ♖b8 0-1**.

16)
Ye Jiangchuan – Bacrot
Europe-Asia rapidplay match, Batumi 2001

Black played **50...e6+!** (50...♖xd5+? 51 ♔e4 costs Black material since his rook and knight are both attacked) **51 ♔e4** (51 ♖xe6 loses the rook after 51...♖xd5+) **51...♘f6+**

52 ♔f3 ♔g7 trapping White's rook and winning the exchange. The finish was **53 ♖xf6 ♔xf6 54 dxe6 ♔xe6 55 ♘f2 ♖c1 56 ♘e4 ♖a1 57 ♘g5+ ♔e7 58 ♔e4 ♖xa2 59 ♔f3 ♖b2 0-1**.

Solutions to Removing the Guard Exercises

1)
Ramirez Alvarez – Chau Sau Ming
Olympiad, Bled 2002

White noticed that the g6-knight has the duty of preventing ♕f8#. He eliminated it directly by **28 ♖xg6** and Black resigned since he faces ruinous material loss.

2)
Oll – Svidler
European Clubs Cup, Kazan 1997

The g2-pawn must prevent ...♕xh3#, so Black eliminated it by **31...♖xg2!**. 32 ♕c3+ ♖8g7 doesn't help White, so he resigned as the only way to avoid a quick mate is to give up almost all his pieces!

3)
Gulko – Benjamin
USA Ch, Chandler 1997

This is a simple case of removing the guard. After **26...♖xe3 27 fxe3 ♘xd2** Black had won two pieces for a rook. The game concluded **28 a4 ♔d7 29 ♖b7 ♖a8 30 ♖b4 ♘e4 31 ♖d1 ♔e6 32 ♖b7 ♖xa4 33 ♖xc7 ♘g5 0-1**.

4)
Van Wely – J. Polgar
Hoogeveen 1997

Removing the guard tactics occur quite often when attacking the king. Here Black was able to force mate by removing the guard of the g3-pawn: **30...♖xf2+** and White resigned in view of 31 ♖xf2 ♕xg3+ 32 ♔f1 ♕xf2#.

5)
Lobzhanidze – Millan Urrutia
Ubeda 2000

White played **25 ♘dc5**, which both uncovers an attack by White's queen on the f5-pawn, and at the same time drives Black's queen away from guarding it. 25...♗xc5 26 ♘xc5 doesn't help Black, and when the queen moves away White will play ♕xf5+ followed by ♕xh7, winning a piece.

6)
Lima – Mellado Trivino
Leon 1997

There is a right way and a wrong way to go about the task of removing the guard of the e6-rook. The wrong way is 20...♗xd4+? since after 21 ♕xd4 White threatens mate on h8, and 21...♕xe6 runs into 22 ♕g7#. The right way is **20...c5!** with a genuine attack on the supporting knight; now White cannot avoid losing material.

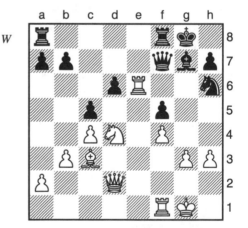

The game continued **21 ♖xd6 cxd4 22 ♗xd4** (White has obtained two pawns for the piece, but they do not provide enough compensation in the long run) **22...♖ad8 23 ♗xa7 ♖xd6 24 ♕xd6 b5 25 ♕d5 ♕xd5 26 cxd5 ♖a8 27 ♗b6 ♖xa2 28 ♖d1 ♘f7 29 d6 ♖a1 30 ♖xa1 ♗xa1 31 d7 ♗f6 32 ♔f2 ♘d8 33 ♔e3 ♔f7 34 ♗xd8 ♗xd8 35 ♔d4 ♔e6 36**

♔c5 h5 37 ♔xb5 ♚xd7 38 ♔c4 h4 39 gxh4 ♗c7 0-1.

7)

Magomedov – Nikolaidis
Koszalin 1999

Black won a pawn by a temporary piece sacrifice: **20...♘eg4! 21 hxg4 ♘xg4** (now White's queen has to quit the defence of the d4-knight) **22 ♕e1** (defending the a1-rook) **22...♕xd4+ 23 ♔h1 g6 24 ♖f4 ♘e5** (Black has won a pawn and in addition has several positional advantages, such as his superb knight on e5 and White's weak pawns; the rest of the game should have been easy) **25 ♖d1 0-0-0 26 b5 cxb5 27 ♕a5** and now 27...g5!, followed by ...♖d6 and ...♖h6+, would have given Black a decisive attack. Black actually played **27...a6**, which also proved sufficient for an eventual win.

8)

Alvarez – Nyback
Bermuda 2002

White found a decisive combination based on the twin themes of removing the guard and discovered check. He started with **24 ♕xh5!**, removing the knight which defends g7.

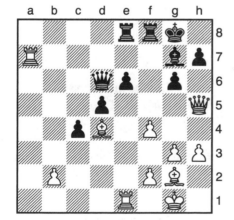

24...♖f7 (a desperate attempt to defend; 24...♗xd4 fails to 25 ♕xh7#, while 24...gxh5

25 ♖xg7+ ♔h8 26 ♖d7+ will leave White at least a piece up) **25 ♖xf7** (25 ♕d1 leaves White a piece up, but the move played is even more forcing) **25...gxh5 26 ♖xg7+ ♔f8 27 ♖xh7** (27 ♖a1 followed by 28 ♖aa7 would have been even quicker) **1-0**. Black had seen enough; in addition to being well down on material (♖+2♗+♙ vs ♕), his king is hopelessly exposed.

Solutions to Opening and Closing Lines Exercises

1)

Kovaliov – K. Rasmussen
Gistrup 1996

After **35 ♘g6+**, Black resigned since it is mate by 35...hxg6 36 ♕h4#. The initial sacrifice opened the h-file ready for White's queen.

2)

Gallagher – Klauser
Swiss Ch, Leukerbad 2002

White won with the line-closing move **24 ♖d6**, when Black resigned in view of inevitable mate on e7 (24...♕xd6 25 ♕xd6 only delays the end by one move).

3)

Kozak – Pisk
Ostrava 2002

White resigned after **30...♖xe3!**. This move threatens mate on g2 or h1, and if White takes the rook he is mated: 31 ♖xe3 ♕h1+ 32 ♔e2 ♕d1#. Mate can only be delayed for at most a few moves if White gives away various pieces. The sacrifice opened the d-file ready for the final mate on d1.

4)

Van Wely – Morozevich
Wijk aan Zee 2001

21...♖g8+! led to instant resignation, as it is mate next move by 22 ♗xg8 ♕g7#. The opening of the line d7-g7 proved fatal for White.

5)

Bologan – Akopian
FIDE Grand Prix, Moscow 2002

Any move by the f3-rook along the third rank threatens mate in two by ...♕f2+ and ...♕h2#, but which square is most effective? Black played **49...♖e3!!**, a spectacular blow which combines the opening of the line f6-f2 with a very unusual 'fork' of White's rooks.

White cannot avoid catastrophe; for example, 50 ♕f1 ♕xe5 and 50 ♖f1 ♕xe5 cost White a rook, while 50 ♖e2 ♖d1+ leads to mate. The game actually finished **50 ♕b7+ ♔h8 51 ♖f1 ♕xe5 52 ♕b6 ♕g5 53 h4 ♕xh4 0-1**. Note that 49...♖b3 is ineffective, since White can defend by 50 ♕c5.

6)

Kovchan – Moiseenko
Kharkov 2002

The game concluded **51...♕g3+!!** (a beautiful sacrifice forcing mate in six; the basic idea is to open the h-file for Black's rooks) **52 ♖xg3 hxg3+** and White resigned due to 53 ♔g2 (53 ♔g4 and 53 ♔xg3 are both met by 53...♖g5#) 53...♖h2+ 54 ♔xg3 (54 ♔f1 ♖f2+ mates after 55 ♔e1 ♖h1# or 55 ♔g1 ♖xc2+

56 ♔f1 ♖h1#) 54...♗f2+ 55 ♔g4 ♖2h4+ 56 ♔f5 ♖8h5#.

Solutions to Back-Rank Mate Exercises

1)

Berezovsky – Singer
German Ch, Altenkirchen 2001

White played the multi-purpose deflection **32 ♕e4!**, which not only stops the mate on g2, but also attacks Black's queen and knight. The queen cannot be taken because of ♖d8+ followed by mate. Black resigned, since although he can defend the knight by 32...♕b8, it doesn't help him as White continues the back-rank theme with 33 ♕xf4, winning a piece.

2)

Yandemirov – Landa
Russia Cup, Omsk 1996

The black knight on e4 controls f2, raising the possibility of a back-rank mate. Black exploited this by **32...♖c7!**; then 33 ♗xd5 and 33 ♗xd7 both allow mate, while 33 ♗b5 ♗xb5 costs White material. 33 ♖xe4+ dxe4 34 ♗xe4 is relatively best, but even this is an easy win for Black after 34...♖c4. White immediately resigned.

3)

Degraeve – Vaïsser
French Ch playoff, Marseilles 2001

White resigned after **46...♕xe3!**, since 47 fxe3 ♖f1# is mate at once, while otherwise Black not only wins a piece for nothing, but also forces a quick mate in any case.

4)

I. Sokolov – de Firmian
Reykjavik 1998

The finish was **40...♕xc5+ 0-1**; this leads to mate in a few moves by 41 ♔h1 (41 ♖xc5

♖xf1#) 41...♘f2+ 42 ♔g1 ♘h3++ 43 ♔h1 ♕g1#.

5)

Sutovsky – de la Riva
Pamplona 1998/9

A back-rank mate may appear unlikely, but the e6-pawn and h6-bishop control the squares f7 and g7 respectively, substituting for black pawns on those squares. Black resigned after **32 ♖xg8+**, since mate is forced: 32...♖xg8 33 ♕xg8+! ♔xg8 34 ♖d8#.

6)

Ribshtein – Volzhin
Budapest 2000

White could have won by 24 ♕xc4! (this does not lead to mate, but it is a back-rank combination all the same) 24...bxc4 25 ♖b8+ (the men blocking in the black king don't have to be pawns; here the queen and bishop prevent the king from fleeing to the second rank) 25...♕d8 (25...♗c8 26 ♖xc8+ costs Black all his pieces) 26 ♖xd8+ ♔xd8 27 ♘e5, winning a piece due to the pin along the d-file.

7)

A. Marić – Kosintseva
European Women's Ch, Varna 2002

White probably hoped to gain material with **43 ♘xd6?** (43 h3 is better, with a likely draw), since both 43...♖xd6 44 ♖xc7 and 43...♖xb7 44 cxb7 are totally winning for White. However, Black replied **43...♖xc6!** and suddenly White was helpless; for example, 44 ♖xc6 ♘e2+ 45 ♔h1 ♖f1# or 44 ♖bb2 ♘e2+ 45 ♖xe2 ♖c1+ 46 ♖e1 ♖xe1#. Faced with ending up a rook down, White decided to resign.

8)

Kharlov – Hulak
European Clubs Cup, Budapest 1996

White broke down Black's remaining resistance on the back rank with a rook sacrifice:

34 ♖g8+! and Black resigned in view of 34...♖xg8 35 ♖xg8+ ♔xg8 36 ♕a8+ ♖e8 37 ♕xe8#.

9)

Tsesarsky – Rotman
Petah Tiqwa 1997

White exploited Black's weak back with **39 ♖xe4! fxe4 40 ♗xe6**, which wins two pieces for a rook since Black cannot reply 40...♖xe6 due to 41 ♖c8+ mating. In the resulting position Black cannot keep his e4-pawn, so White ends up with two very active bishops in return for a rook. This proved sufficient for a win: **40...h6 41 ♗d5 ♖be7 42 ♗xe4 ♔g8 43 ♗d5+ ♔h7 44 ♗e4+ ♔g8 45 ♗g6 ♖a8 46 h4 ♖ea7 47 ♗e4 ♖d8 48 ♔g4 ♖ad7 49 ♖c6 ♔f7 50 ♔h5 ♔g8 51 ♗f5 ♖e7 52 ♔g6 ♖de8 53 ♖d6 ♖b8 54 ♗e6+ ♔f8 55 ♖a6 1-0**. In the final position Black must lose more material as both ♗xb8 and ♗d6 are threatened.

10)

Liu Dede – Isaev
Asian Ch, Calcutta 2001

Two moves were enough to destroy Black's position: **29 ♕e8+!** (the first blow; White's queen cannot be taken as 29...♖xe8 30 ♖xe8+ ♗f8 31 ♖xf8# is mate) **29...♗f8 30 ♕f7!** (the second blow; 31 ♕g8# is threatened, and if 30...♗c5 then 31 ♖e8+ mates) **30...♗e7 31 ♖xe7 1-0**. Black faces a ruinous material loss.

11)

Rozentalis – Adams
Olympiad, Elista 1998

With 30 ♗xf5 White was hoping to escape from his difficult position by exchanging bishops and then queens. However, he was rocked back by the reply **30...♕xe1+!**. After 31 ♖xe1 ♘xf5 32 ♖xe8+ ♖xe8 White's queen cannot move so as to guard the threatened back-rank mate on e1. It follows that there is nothing better than 33 ♘d3, but after

33...♘xg3+ 34 hxg3 ♖e2 the ending is an easy win. White therefore resigned.

12)
V. Georgiev – Lazarev
Elgoibar 1999

Congratulations if you managed to solve this rather difficult exercise! Various tactical ideas based on Black's weak back rank play a part in the solution. The game continued **34 ♕d4!** (this deflection allows White to transfer his queen to the eighth rank with gain of tempo) **34...♕a3** (the deflection is not immediately decisive as Black still has a square to maintain his defence of f8) **35 ♕d8 ♔g8** (the only way to defend the attacked rook) **36 ♕d5+** (another tempo-gaining move, allowing the queen to switch to f7) **36...♔h8 37 ♕f7!** (White again doubly attacks the poor f8-rook, and this time there is no ...♔g8 to defend it) **37...♕d6+** (there is no real defence; Black can only delay the end slightly by giving a couple of checks) **38 f4 ♕h6+ 39 ♔g3 1-0**.

Solutions to Pawn Promotion Exercises

1)
de la Villa – Illescas
Pamplona 1999/00

Following **36...♗h5!** White resigned, because after 37 ♗xh5 bxc2 the black pawn promotes, while otherwise White loses his bishop.

2)
Bobras – Lagowski
Polish Ch, Warsaw 2002

White continued **53 ♗a5+!** and Black resigned since after 53...♔xa5 54 a7 the a-pawn promotes, while otherwise Black loses his bishop. Here White decisively combined the ideas of pawn promotion and skewer.

3)
Drogoon – Gorbatov
Russia Cup, Moscow 1998

White won with **49 ♗d5!**. This bishop is immune from capture (49...♗xd5 50 e8♕# or 49...♖xd5 50 b8♕+ followed by mate) and by pinning the f7-bishop, White threatens 50 e8♕#. There is nothing Black can do apart from 49...♖b2+, but after 50 ♔g1 ♖b1+ 51 ♔f2 ♖b2+ 52 ♔e3 the checks come to an end and Black faces imminent defeat. He therefore resigned at once.

4)
Hebden – Hanley
British Ch, Torquay 2002

When an advanced pawn is blockaded by an enemy piece, one way of shifting the blockade is to concentrate all one's firepower on the blockading piece. Black resigned after **39 ♕e8+! ♗f8 40 ♖b8**, when the multiple attack on the d8-rook leaves Black helpless (40...♖xb8 41 ♕xb8 and the pawn will promote).

5)
Hector – Åkesson
Nordic Ch, Reykjavik 1997

White won a piece with a neat combination based on the promotion of his h7-pawn: **39 ♖g8! ♖xg8** (39...♘xg8 loses to 40 ♕xh8 as the g8-knight is pinned) **40 ♕xe7+!** (deflecting Black's queen away from the promotion square) **40...♔c8** (40...♕xe7 41 hxg8♕ also leaves White a piece up) **41 hxg8♕ 1-0**.

6)
Ma. Tseitlin – Psakhis
Israeli Ch, Ramat Aviv/Modiin 2000

Black won by playing **26...exf3! 27 ♖xc7 f2**. White's pieces are unable to prevent the promotion on f1 (for example, 28 ♕d1 ♘g3+ followed by ...f1♕) and so Black's combination nets him a whole rook. As he was a piece down to start with, Black ends up the exchange ahead. The finish was **28 ♔h2 f1♕**

29 ♕h3 ♖f7 30 ♖xf7 ♔xf7 31 ♕xh7+ ♘g7 32 ♘b7 ♕f6 33 ♘d6+ ♔e6 34 ♔g1 ♖b8 35 ♗e1 ♖b1 36 ♕g8+ ♔e5 0-1.

7)

Ki. Georgiev – Henrichs
Recklinghausen 1998

Black should have played 33...a6, with a likely draw. Instead he preferred **33...a5?**, but resigned after the reply **34 axb5!**. If 34...axb4 then 35 b6 promotes the pawn, while after 34...cxb5 (relatively the best) 35 ♖xb5 Black loses his a-pawn as well, whereupon he is the exchange down for nothing.

8)

Nieto – Blit
Argentine Under-12 Ch, Esperanza 2002

It is tempting to play 22...bxa2, but after 23 ♘a3 White rounds up the advanced a2-pawn, leaving Black with only a modest advantage. Instead, Black found the far more effective continuation **22...♕xa2!** (trapping the rook on a1!) **23 ♖xa2 bxa2**. White cannot prevent promotion, so Black emerges a rook ahead. The finish was **24 ♘a3 a1♕ 25 ♗f6 gxf6 26 exf6 ♖b7 27 ♕g5+ ♔h8 28 ♗h5 ♘d8 29 ♕h4 ♕c1 30 g4 ♘f7 31 ♗xf7 ♖xf7 32 ♕h5 ♖xf6 0-1.**

9)

M. Röder – Senoner
Graz 1997

If Black simply recaptures on c6, then White moves his rook from b1 and remains a piece up. 17...axb1♕ is equally ineffective because after 18 ♘xd8 Black's newly-created queen is trapped, and after 18...♕xf1+ 19 ♗xf1 ♖fxd8 20 exd6 White has a decisive material advantage. The winning move is **17...axb1♘!**. Here the motivation for the knight promotion is that a knight on b1 attacks White's queen, whereas a queen on b1 would not. However White plays, he ends up down on material; for example, 18 ♘xd8 ♘xd2 19 ♘xb7 ♘xf1 leaves Black two exchanges up,

while after 18 ♖xb1 ♗xc6 White is the exchange and a pawn down. The game continuation was **18 ♘xe7+ ♕xe7 19 exd6 ♘xd2 20 dxe7 ♖fe8 21 ♖d1 ♘xc4 22 ♖xd7 ♘xb2** and Black won with his extra rook.

10)

Rogers – Van de Mortel
Wijk aan Zee 1995

At present material is more or less balanced (rook and pawn for bishop and knight) but White tipped the balance decisively in his favour with the simple but unexpected pinning move **28 ♕h6!**. White threatens 29 h8♕+, and 28...♔f7 fails to 29 ♕e6+ ♔f8 30 ♕g8#. Black was reduced to **28...♗xh6**, but he resigned after **29 h8♕+ ♔f7 30 ♕xh6 e5 31 ♘f3** since he is not only a whole exchange down, but in addition his king remains very exposed.

11)

V. Georgiev – Paramos Dominguez
Skopje 2002

In fact 42 ♗g5? is bad, because after 42...♗f6 White's d-pawn is definitely kept under control, while he faces material loss along the g-file. In this case he could hope for a draw at most. Instead, White won by trusting in the d-pawn: **42 ♕xg6! hxg6 43 ♗g5!** (this is the right way to push the pawn home; after 43 ♗b6? ♗f6 44 ♖f1 White threatens to win with 45 d8♕ or 45 ♖xf6, but Black can defend by 44...♕h6 45 ♖xf6 ♕g5+ with perpetual check, since if the king moves to the f-file the rook drops with check) **43...♕xb4** (43...♗f6 44 ♗xf6 ♕xf6 45 ♖a8+ followed by 46 d8♕ also leaves White a rook up) **44 d8♕+ 1-0**.

12)

Short – Stefansson
Match (game 5), Reykjavik 2002

Even if you have a good move available, it is often worth spending a little time looking for a better one. White would undoubtedly have good winning chances after 38 exf8♕+, but his modest material advantage (rook for bishop and pawn) might not be so easy to convert into the full point. White actually played **38 ♖xg6+!** and Black resigned in view of 38...hxg6 (38...fxg6 39 exf8♕#) 39 h7+, when White ends up a queen ahead: 39...♔xh7 40 exf8♕ or 39...♔g7 40 exf8♕+ ♔xf8 41 h8♕+.

13)

Terentiev – Gallagher
Liechtenstein 1990

No, it wasn't correct as White had over-looked a pawn-promotion combination. The game (which started **1 d4 ♘f6 2 ♗g5 ♘e4 3 ♗f4 c5 4 c3 ♕b6 5 ♕b3 cxd4 6 ♕xb6 axb6**) continued **7 ♗xb8?** (7 cxd4 is better, although Black still has some advantage due to his better development) **7...dxc3 8 ♗e5?** (this is really disastrous; 8 ♘xc3 ♘xc3 9 bxc3 ♖xb8 leaves White a pawn down, but anything is better than what happened now!) **8...♖xa2!**.

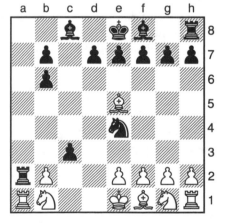

A brilliant and unexpected blow; after 9 ♖xa2 c2 the pawn promotes, so White is forced to jettison material. **9 ♘xc3 ♖xa1+ 10 ♘d1 ♘xf2 11 ♔xf2 ♖xd1** (the exchange and three pawns down, White could well have resigned here, but he plays on to the bitter end)

12 e3 e6 13 ♗e2 ♖c1 14 h4 ♗b4 15 h5 f6 16 ♗d4 e5 17 ♗xb6 d5 18 g3 ♗f5 19 ♖h4 ♗e1+ 20 ♔g2 ♗e4+ 21 ♗f3 ♖c2+ 22 ♔h3 f5 0-1.

14)

Frieser – U. Böhm
Germany (Oberliga) 1993/4

It looks as though Black should resign, since giving his king some air by 24...b6 fails to 25 ♘d6+ ♔d7 26 ♘f5+ winning the queen. Amazingly, the position is winning for Black! The game continued **24...♕c5+!** (the only move, but a strong one) **25 ♔g2** (25 ♔h1 loses at once to 25...♕xc1+, while after 25 ♖xc5 e1♕+ 26 ♔g2 ♕e2+ followed by ...♕xd3 there is no mate and Black wins with his extra material) **25...e1♘+!** (again forced; Black must meet the threat of 26 ♖d8#, and 25...♘e7 loses to 26 ♘d6+, as 26...♔d7 27 ♘xb7+ costs Black his queen while 26...♔xc7 allows White to take the queen with check).

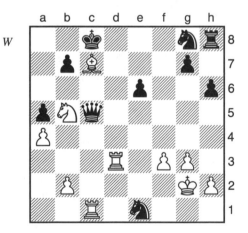

26 ♖xe1 (if White moves his king, then 26...♘xd3 27 ♖xc5 ♘xc5 leaves Black a rook up) **26...♕c2+** (the final point: the d3-rook falls and Black secures a decisive material advantage) **27 ♔g1 ♕xd3 28 ♗f4 ♘e7 29 ♘d6+ ♔d7 30 ♘f7 ♘g6 31 ♘xh8 ♘xh8 32 ♗e5 ♘f7 33 ♗xg7 ♘g5 34 ♖f1 ♕e2 0-1**. This was a difficult exercise and anyone who found Black's first two moves can be justly proud.

Solutions to In-Between Moves Exercises

1)
Kyaw Kyaw Soe – Dang Tat Thang
Zonal tournament, Yangon 1998

After **27 ♗xc5** Black resigned, because 27...♕xd1 28 ♗xe7+ (the in-between move) 28...♔xe7 29 ♘xd1 leaves White a piece up for nothing.

2)
Cvitan – Khuzman
European Ch, Ohrid 2001

In fact **31...♖xe2?** was a losing mistake (Black should have continued 31...♕d7, although White retains a considerable advantage even after this). Although the lines 32 ♘xf5? ♖xd2 and 32 ♕xe2? ♕xf2 favour Black, the in-between move **32 ♗xg7+!** destroyed his hopes. After 32...♔xg7 33 ♘xf5+ or 32...♔e8/e7 33 ♕xe2+ White delivers a crucial check, winning the enemy queen in both cases. Faced with heavy material loss, Black resigned.

3)
Andonovski – Bojković
Skopje 2002

No, Black has a much stronger move than simply recapturing on d6. The game continued **18...♘h4+!** (a fork combined with possible deflection of the g3-pawn) **19 ♔h1** (19 gxh4 ♘f4+ 20 ♔h1 ♘xe2 wins White's queen for insufficient material) **19...♘xf3** (White must lose material, since both e1 and d6 are under attack) **20 ♘e4 ♘xe1 21 ♖xe1** (Black has won the exchange for nothing, and White soon decided to give up) **21...♘f6! 22 f3 ♘xe4 23 fxe4 ♖f7 24 ♕g4 ♗xc4 25 bxc4 ♖af8 0-1**.

4)
Singh – Aarthie
Calcutta 2002

White struck with the in-between move **31 ♕xe8+!**. Black resigned since White emerges a piece up after 31...♕f8 32 ♕xf8+ ♖xf8 33 bxc3 or a queen up after 31...♖xe8 32 ♖xe8+ ♕g8 33 ♖xg8+ ♔xg8 34 d6+ (of course 34 bxc3 is also good enough to win) followed by 35 dxc7.

Solutions to Defensive Tactics Exercises

1)
Halkias – Dambacher
Lost Boys, Amsterdam 2002

The position is winning for White, and after 66 ♕e6+ followed by 67 ♔f5, for example, Black would lose in the long run. However, White wanted to win immediately and carelessly played **66 ♔f5?**, threatening mate on g6 and apparently forcing Black to exchange queens by 66...♕h7+. However, Black actually continued **66...♕f7+!** and after the forced **67 ♕xf7** it was stalemate.

2)
del Rio – Illescas
Dos Hermanas 2002

58 ♔f5? was a mistake because of the continuation **58...♖xa7! 59 ♖xa7** with stalemate. White could have won easily in the diagram position by 58 ♔d6 heading for the a-pawn and winning Black's rook within a few moves.

3)
Dittmar – Schulte
Dresden 2002

Of course this position is totally winning for Black, but even with such an overwhelming advantage it is still possible to make a mistake. Black played **50...♔g5??** and was doubtless shocked by the continuation **51 ♖g4+! ♔xg4** stalemate. The lesson here is that concentration is necessary right up to the moment that your opponent resigns.

4)
Prokopchuk – Smirin
Moscow 2002

Evidently White thought so, because he played **20 ♕d2?**. However, after the reply **20...♕c3!** he had to resign, since Black keeps his extra piece (21 ♕xc3 ♘xe2+ 22 ♔h1 ♘xc3). Instead White should have played 20 ♕xa1 ♘xe2+ 21 ♔h1 ♗xa1 22 ♖xa1, when he has some drawing chances.

5)
Sagalchik – Kaufman
USA Ch, Seattle 2002

Had White been a little more patient then he would have secured the win; for example, after 25 ♖xe8+ ♕xe8 26 ♕a6, attacking the f6-pawn, White wins easily. However, the move played, **25 ♖1d7??**, was a terrible blunder because Black replied with the deflection **25...♕xd7**. White loses a rook and so **he** was the one who had to resign.

6)
Janković – Tomicić
Croatian Under-18 Team Ch, Pula 2002

In the game Black played **64...♖xg2?**, but White drew by **65 ♖b3+ f3** (65...♔f2 even loses, to 66 ♖b2+) **66 ♖xf3+! gxf3** (66...♔xf3 is also stalemate) with stalemate. He could have won by 64...f3! 65 gxf3 ♖h2+ 66 ♔g1 gxf3; for example, 67 ♖b3 ♖a2 68 ♖b1 ♖g2+ 69 ♔f1 ♖h2 70 ♔g1 f2+ 71 ♔f1 ♖h1+ and White's rook falls.

7)
Lawrenz – H. Ernst
Bad Ragaz 1994

White saved the game with the surprising **31 ♖d8!**. This threatens both 32 ♕xe7 and 32 ♖xc8, so **31...♕xh4** was forced, but then

White gave perpetual check by **32 ♖xf8+ ♔h7 33 ♖xf7+** ½-½.

8)
Bobotsov – Petrosian
Moscow 1967

White saved the game by playing for perpetual check: **19 ♗h3! ♗xe2 20 ♗xh7+ ♔h8** and a draw was agreed as White can repeat moves by 21 ♗g6+ (or anywhere else on the same diagonal) 21...♔g8 22 ♗h7+, etc.

9)
Smirin – Tukmakov
Solin 1999

White's position looks very poor, since Black's pawn is on the verge of promotion. In the game he tried pinning the pawn by **69 ♕f3?**, but lost after **69...♕d4 70 ♔a2 ♔d2 71 ♕g2 ♕a7+ 72 ♔b2 ♕d4+ 73 ♔a2 ♕e5 74 b4 ♔d3 75 ♕f3+ ♕e3 76 ♕d5+ ♕d4 77 ♕f3+ ♔d2 78 ♕g2 ♕xb4 79 ♕f2 ♕c4+ 80 ♔b2 ♕c3+ 0-1**. After 81 ♔b1 or 81 ♔a2, Black plays 81...♔d1 and White can no longer prevent promotion. However, in the diagram position White missed an immediate draw by 69 ♕h1+! e1♕ (69...♕e1 70 ♕d5+ repeats) 70 ♕f3+ (70 ♕h5+ also draws) 70...♕de2 71 ♕d5+ ♕1d2 72 ♕h1+ ♕ee1 73 ♕f3+ and Black cannot evade the checks.

10)
Kharlov – Nisipeanu
Ljubljana 2002

White used the discovered-attack motif to rescue his attacked pieces: **26 ♗d6!** and Black resigned because after 26...♖xd6 27 ♗xf7+ ♔xf7 28 ♖xd6 White is the exchange and a pawn ahead with an easy win.

11)
R. Mainka – Stefanova
Recklinghausen 1998

The game finished **40...♔e7? 41 ♖b7+** (now White can deliver perpetual check) **41...♔f8** (41...♔d8 42 ♘f7+ followed by

♘d6+ is also perpetual check, since 42...♔e8 43 ♘d6+ ♔f8?? runs into 44 ♖f7#) **42 ♖b8+ ♔e7 43 ♖b7+ ♔f8** (43...♔f6?? 44 ♖f7#) **44 ♖b8+ ♔g7 45 ♖b7+ ♔f8 46 ♖b8+ ♔e7 47 ♖b7+ ♔e8 48 ♖b8+ ½-½.** 40...♔c7? is also wrong, as White draws by 41 ♘f3+! (shielding the f4-bishop from the attack of Black's queen) 41...e5 42 ♗xe5+ ♔d7 43 ♗xf5+ ♔e7 44 ♖b7+ and there is no escape from the rook checks. The winning move is 40...♔d6!, which looks least likely because it allows White to give a double check. However, after 41 ♘f3+ ♔d5 or 41 ♘c4++ ♔d5 the checks soon run out, whereupon Black wins easily with her massive material advantage.

12)

Dorfman – Onishchuk
Cap d'Agde 2000

Yes, Black could have improved. After **73 ♗xf6 ♔xf6 74 ♖a6+ ♔g7 75 ♖a7+** he could have drawn by 75...♔f6!. If White takes the rook it is stalemate, while 76 ♖a6+ ♔g7 simply repeats the position. Curiously not only Onishchuk, but also Grandmaster Ribli, annotating the game in *ChessBase Magazine*, overlooked this drawing resource.

13)

Benitah – Cvitan
Mitropa Cup, Baden 1999

Black started with **52...f3+!**. If now 53 ♔h3 g2 54 h8♕ g1♕, the question is whether White has a perpetual check. The answer is no, but Black must take care not to capture the b6-pawn, since then White would be able to force stalemate by giving up his queen. One line runs 55 ♕c8+ ♔d6 56 ♕c7+ ♔e6 57 ♕c6+ ♔e7 58 ♕c7+ ♔f6 59 ♕d6+ ♔f5 60 ♕d7+ ♔g5 61 ♕d8+ ♔f4 62 ♕f6+ ♔e4 63 ♕c6+ ♔e3 64 ♕c3+ ♔f4 65 ♕d2+ ♗e3 66 ♕b4+ ♔f5 and the checks run out. Therefore White played **53 ♔xf3**, and the game ended **53...♗d4!** (setting up the discovered attack 54 h8♕ e4+) **54 ♔e4** (forced to prevent Black advancing the e-pawn) **54...f5+!**

(removing the blockading king) **55 ♔xf5 e4 56 ♔xe4 g2 0-1**.

14)

Wintzer – Von Gleich
Saint Augustin 1990

White solved the problem by forcing a surprising perpetual check: **22 ♗xh7+! ♔xh7 23 ♕xg7+! ♔xg7 24 ♖g3+ ♔h8 25 ♖h3+ ♔g8 26 ♖g3+ ½-½** (this possibility was first pointed out in analysis of the famous game Ljubojević-Andersson, Wijk aan Zee 1976).

15)

Gretarsson – Ashley
Bermuda 1999

After **27...♘f2?**, White replied **28 ♕xe2 dxe2 29 ♗xf2**, defusing Black's attack and remaining with the material advantage of two rooks and a knight (13 points) for a queen and a pawn (10 points). In the game continuation White was able to free his pieces and move over to the attack: **29...♕e5 30 ♖e1 f5 31 c4 ♕c7 32 ♖xe2 ♕xc4 33 ♔h2 ♕xd5 34 ♖c1 f4 35 ♔g1 h5 36 ♘f3 g4 37 ♖d2 ♕b5 38 hxg4 hxg4 39 ♘e5 ♗f5 40 ♖d8+ ♔h7 41 ♖c7+ ♔h6 42 ♖h8+ 1-0**. However, in the diagram position Black could have forced a draw and it is curious that neither Ashley nor annotator Avrukh (in *ChessBase Magazine*) spotted it. The saving move for Black is 27...♗a4!!.

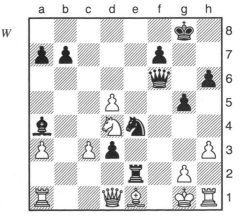

White has to take care not to lose, but after the best reply 28 ♕xd3 (28 ♕b1 ♗c2! and 28 ♕c1 d2 can only favour Black, while after 28 ♕xa4? ♖xe1+! 29 ♖xe1 ♕f2+ 30 ♔h2 ♕g3+ 31 ♔g1 ♕xe1+ 32 ♔h2 ♕g3+ 33 ♔g1 ♕e3+ 34 ♔h2 ♘xc3! Black has decisive threats) 28...♖xe1+! 29 ♖xe1 ♕f2+ 30 ♔h2 ♕f4+ the game ends in perpetual check.

16)

Hnydiuk – Tyomkin
European Junior Ch, Tallinn 1997

Clearly there is a stalemate if White can get rid of his queen, but the stalemate only exists while Black's king is blocking the g4-pawn. Consequently White has to choose the correct check here, because once the opportunity has gone it won't turn up again. The right move is 88 ♕e5+!!. Then 88...♔h4 and 88...♔h6 allow 89 ♕xf6+ followed by ♕b2 with an easy draw, while 88...♔xg4 89 ♕e2+ ♕xe2 is stalemate. That leaves just 88...♔g6, but after 89 ♕e8+ ♔h6 90 ♕e3+ ♔g7 91 ♕e7+ ♔g6 92 ♕e8+ Black can only repeat the position. In the game White played 88 ♕e3+? but now Black is winning. He can evade the checks without capturing the g4-pawn, and then White is lost: **88...♔h4!**.

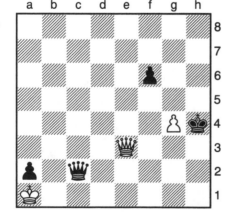

89 ♕e1+ (89 ♕g5+ ♔g3 90 ♕e3+ ♔g2 and Black wins) **89...♔h3 90 ♕h1+ ♔g3 91**
♕g1+ ♔f3 92 ♕f1+ (92 ♕h1+ ♔f4 is much the same) **92...♔e3 93 ♕e1+ ♔f4 94 ♕f1+** (94 ♕b4+ is a better chance, setting the trap 94...♔g5? 95 ♕d2+!, but after 94...♔e4! Black reaches a winning ending with ♕+f♙ vs ♕) **94...♔g5 95 ♕b5+ ♔h4 96 ♕g5+ ♔g3 97 ♕e3+ ♔g2 98 ♕e1 ♕b1+ 99 ♕xb1 axb1♕+ 100 ♔xb1 ♔g3 101 ♔c2 ♔xg4 102 ♔d2 ♔f3 103 ♔e1 f5 0-1**. After 104 ♔f1 f4 White must allow ...♔e2 or ...♔g2, whereupon the pawn promotes.

Solutions to Combinations Exercises

1)

Karaklajić – Zhang Zhong
Beijing 1997

The finish was **37...♘xd4+** and White resigned since he loses his queen.

2)

Varga – Anastasian
World Team Ch, Erevan 2001

White combined a fork with the deflection motif to win by **46 ♘e8+**. After 46...♖xe8 47 ♖xd7 Black loses even more material because of the fork of c7 and f7, so he resigned.

3)

Joecks – Shabalov
Hamburg 1999

Black ignored the attacked bishop and played **20...h5**. Now 21 ♕xg5 ♘h3+ and 21 ♕g3 ♘e2+ lose the queen to knight forks, so White played **21 ♕f5**. However, after **21...g6** the queen was trapped in mid-board.

4)

Grabarczyk – Bobras
Polish Ch, Warsaw 2002

White played **25 ♘d6!**, exploiting the pin of the rook, and trapping Black's queen.

Black resigned in view of the impending material loss.

5)

Short – Leko
Sarajevo 1999

White's b-pawn is pinned, and so Black was able to play **44...♖c3**, trapping White's queen.

6)

Smirin – Pelletier
Biel 2002

White won a piece by **28 ♕xe6**, since after 28...♖xe6 29 ♘f7+ the deflection allows a knight fork regaining the queen.

7)

Plachetka – Berkes
Mitropa Cup, Leipzig 2002

A combination of pawn promotion and back-rank mate led to victory for Black after **29...♖a1!**. 30 ♖xa1 c1♕+ 31 ♖xc1 ♖xc1# is mate, while 30 fxe3 ♖xc1+ 31 ♔f2 ♖f1+ followed by ...c1♕ gives Black an extra queen, so White resigned.

8)

Kinsić – Yilmaz
European Team Ch, Batumi 2002

White played the surprising move **35 ♖f8!** threatening both to take on g8 and to win the queen by 36 ♘g6+. Black faces heavy loss of material and could find nothing better than **35...♖xf8 36 ♘g6+ ♔g7 37 ♘xh4+ ♗xg3 38 hxg3**, but White's extra material proved decisive: **38...♔f6 39 ♔f2 ♖c8 40 ♗d4+ ♔g5 41 ♗c3 ♔g4 42 ♘f5 ♖f8 43 ♔e3 h5 44 ♗g7 ♖d8 45 ♗f6 ♖d7 46 ♔f2 ♔h3 47 d4 ♖f7 48 e5 dxe5 49 dxe5 ♖f8 50 ♔f3 b6 51 axb6 ♖b8 52 e6 ♖xb6 53 ♘g7 a5 54 ♗c3 ♖b7 55 ♘f5 ♖b6 56 e7 ♖e6 57 ♔f4 a4 58 ♗b4 ♖e2 59 ♘e3 ♖xb2 60 ♗d6 a3 61 e8♕ a2 62 ♕xh5#**. Note that the immediate 35 ♘g6+? is bad due to 35...♖xg6 36 ♖xg6 ♕e1+ winning the bishop.

9)

Kasparov – Adams
Sarajevo 1999

White continued **30 ♖xe8+ ♖xe8 31 ♖d1** and Black resigned as 31...♕e2 is the only way to avoid loss of the b5-knight, but then comes the skewer 32 ♖e1 and Black loses material.

10)

Shirov – Motylev
FIDE Knockout (rapid playoff), Moscow 2001

White won by a combination of skewer and back-rank mate: **13 ♖xb2!** (the similar idea 13 ♕a4+ ♘d7 14 ♖xb2 is equally effective) **1-0**. Both 13...♕xa6 14 ♖xb8+ ♕c8 15 ♖xc8# and 13...♕xb2 14 ♕c6+ ♔d8 15 ♘xf7# lead to mate.

11)

Putzbach – M. Kopylov
Hamburg 2001

White played **36 ♘dxf6+** (36 ♘exf6+ is equally effective) and Black resigned since he loses his queen after 36...gxf6 37 ♘xf6+.

12)

Rublevsky – Varga
World Team Ch, Erevan 2001

White won by deflection combined with line-opening: **14 ♗f4! ♕xf4** (Black decides to give up his queen; 14...e5 15 ♗xe5 ♕xe5 16 ♗g6# and 14...♕d7 15 ♗xc7 ♕xc7 16 ♗g6# are even worse) **15 ♗g6+ ♕f7 16 ♗xf7+ ♔xf7** (White is well ahead on material and Black is still troubled by his exposed king) **17 f3! g3 18 ♕d4 ♔g8 19 ♕e5 ♘ba6 20 ♕xg3+ ♗g7 21 ♘c3 ♔f7 22 ♕f4+ ♔e8 23 ♖ad1 ♖c8 24 ♕g5 ♔f7 25 ♘e4 1-0**.

13)

Cherniaev – Motylev
Chigorin memorial, St Petersburg 1999

Black's attack struck first by **20...♖d2+!** 21 ♘xd2 (21 ♗xd2 ♘xc3+ also costs White his queen, while 21 ♔e1 ♕g3+ 22 ♔f1 ♖f2+ is devastating) **21...♘xc3+ 22 ♔d3 ♘xa4** (White could have given up here) **23 ♖af1 ♕d5+ 24 ♔e2 ♘c3+ 25 ♔e1 ♕d3 0-1**.

14)
Kariakin – Kosteniuk
Match (game 4), Brissago 2003

At first sight White has nothing better than 34 ♗a4, but **34 ♖a8!** is decisive. Black loses either the exchange after 34...♗xb3 35 ♖xa6 or a piece after 34...♖xa8 35 ♗xd5+, so she resigned.

15)
Jaracz – Grabarczyk
Polish Ch, Sopot 1997

We have seen the pin plus fork combination several times already and here is another example. White won Black's queen and the game: **19 ♘b6+ ♔c7 20 ♘a6+ ♔d6 21 ♘xb8 ♘xg2+ 22 ♔f2 1-0**.

16)
Komarov – Razuvaev
Reggio Emilia 1996/7

White won as follows: **15 ♖xg7+! ♔xg7** (15...♔h8 16 ♖g6! hxg6 17 ♕h4+ also wins the black queen) **16 ♕g4+** (a discovered attack, which also uses a pin to prevent ...♕g6) **16...♔h8 17 ♗xf6+ ♖xf6 18 ♘g5** (White has a decisive material advantage) **18...♘d7 19 ♘xe6 ♖g6 20 ♕d4+ ♘7f6 21 ♘f4 ♘xf4 22 ♕xf4 bxa3 23 ♕f3 ♗g4 24 ♕xc6 ♖c8 25 ♕a4 ♖e8 26 ♖xa3 ♗xe2 27 ♖e3 ♖xe3 28 fxe3 ♗xf1 29 ♔xf1 h6 30 ♕d4 1-0**.

17)
Benjamin – Ni Hua
USA-China Summit, Shanghai 2002

White won material with a skewer combined with an in-between move: **24 ♘d6! ♕xe2** (after 24...♕xg3 25 ♘xe8+ ♗xe8 26 hxg3 White wins the exchange) **25 ♘xe8+ ♕xe8** (25...♖xe8 26 ♖xe2 ♖xe2 27 ♕c7+ and White picks up the bishop) **26 ♖xe8**

♗xe8 27 ♕b8 (White's queen makes a meal of Black's queenside) **27...gxf5 28 ♕xa7+ ♗f7 29 ♕xb6 ♖e8 30 a4 ♗d5 31 ♕a7+ ♗f7 32 a5 1-0**.

18)
Shipov – Yurtaev
Chigorin memorial, St Petersburg 1997

First White pinned the d6-knight with gain of tempo by **37 ♕b8+ ♔h7** and then he forked Black's king and rook by **38 ♗f5+**. The finish was **38...♕xf5 39 ♖xf5 ♘xf5 40 ♕f4 g6 41 g4 ♘g7 42 d6 1-0**.

19)
Flear – G. Wall
British Ch, Torquay 2002

A combination of skewer and deflection finished Black off: **33 ♖b1!** and Black resigned, because 33...♕xb1 34 ♖xg7+ leads to mate, while if the queen moves away then ♖b8+ is decisive. Black can try 33...♘f2+, but it doesn't help after 34 ♔g2.

20)
Epishin – Felgaer
Linares open 2001

Black resigned after **25 ♗f5!**, as 25...gxf5 26 ♕g5+ mates, while otherwise the skewer of Black's rooks wins the exchange.

21)
Petrov – Kempinski
European Ch, Ohrid 2001

The spectacular deflection move **39...♘c4!** decided the game. The only way to prevent promotion is by 40 ♕xc4, but then the mate threat is relieved and Black wins by 40...♕b2, threatening to promote with check. White therefore resigned.

22)
Feoktistov – Riazantsev
Russian Ch, Elista 2001

It would be mate by ...♕e4+ if only Black could deflect White's bishop from d3. A preliminary line-opening converted Black's wish into reality: **26...♘xe5! 27 dxe5 ♗xb5 28 ♗xa7** (28 ♗xb5 ♕e4+ mates) **28...♗xd3 29 ♕xd3 ♕c1+** (White's king is exposed and his pawns are falling) **30 ♗g1 ♕xb2 31 ♕g3 ♕e2 32 ♗f2 ♗h4! 0-1**. White loses more material since 33 ♕xh4 fails to 33...♕f1+ 34 ♗g1 ♕f3#.

23)
Karasik – V. Mikhalevski
Beersheba 1998

Black combined a fork with a back-rank mate: **22...♗c2! 23 ♕f1** (White must give up a piece, since 23 ♕xc2 ♕xc2 24 ♖xc2 ♖d1# is mate) **23...♗xa4 24 f4 ♘d4 25 c5 ♗c6 26 ♕f2 ♘f5 27 h3 ♘h4 0-1**. After 28 ♕xh4, Black wins by 28...♖xd2 29 ♗xd2 ♕xg2#.

24)
Hochgräfe – Pelletier
Hamburg 1998

White played **17 ♘xd5** and Black resigned, since he cannot avoid heavy material loss. The main point is that 17...♘xd5 18 ♕g4! (but not 18 ♕xd5?? ♗h2+ winning White's queen) leads to mate in a few moves (for example, 18...g6 19 ♘h6#). Relatively best is 17...♗h2+ 18 ♔xh2 ♕xd5, but after 19 ♘d6 ♖cd8 20 ♘xb7 Black is two pawns down with a bad position.

25)
P.H. Nielsen – Kariakin
Hastings 2002/3

Black resigned after **20 ♕a5+**, because 20...♕b6 (20...♔e8 21 d7+) 21 ♖b1! skewers the queen against the back-rank mate on b8.

26)
Mariasin – Zalkind
Israeli Ch, Jerusalem 1996

The sacrifice **31 ♖xd6!** shattered Black's defences: **31...♗xd6** (31...♕xd6 32 ♕xc8+ ♗d8 33 ♘e6+, forking king, rook and bishop, is decisive) **32 ♘e6+** (thanks to the pin, White

wins Black's queen) **32...♔e7 33 ♘xd8 ♔xd8 34 ♖d1 ♖d7 35 ♕c6 ♗b7 36 ♕b6+ ♔e7 37 ♖xd6 1-0**.

27)
Solozhenkin – Norri
Finnish Cht 1993

White won with an unusual combination: **12 ♘xd5!** (12 ♘b5 is also good, but less strong than this move) **12...♕xd5** (12...♕xd2 13 ♘xe7#) **13 c4!** (trapping Black's queen) **13...♘e4** (Black tries to escape, but to no avail) **14 fxe4** and Black resigned, since after 14...♕xe4+ 15 ♗d3 Black loses his queen after all.

28)
Herrera – Abreu
Capablanca memorial, Havana 1998

White won by opening the line e2-b5 with gain of tempo: **21 ♖xe4! ♕b6** (Black decides to surrender the piece, since 21...fxe4 22 ♗b5+ followed by 23 ♘c6+ costs him his queen, but he gives up after a few more moves) **22 ♖e3 b3 23 a3 ♗c5 24 ♖g3 ♖b8 25 c3 1-0**.

29)
G. Kuzmin – Czebe
European Ch, Ohrid 2001

Black struck with **38...♘g6!** and suddenly White, who had been a pawn up, was lost. The game continued **39 ♖g4** (39 ♖h6 ♘f4+ and 39 ♗xg6 ♖xe2+ 40 ♔f3 ♖xa2 are also hopeless for White) **39...f5!** (there is no escape from the various forks and pins, so White must lose material) **40 ♖xg6 ♖xg6 41 ♗d3 ♖xe2+ 42 ♗xe2 a5** and Black was the exchange up for a pawn, which is sufficient to win in the current position. Black did indeed secure the full point, although not in the most efficient manner possible: **43 a4 ♔g7 44 ♗b5 ♔f6 45 ♔f3 ♖g4 46 h4 ♖b4 47 ♗d7 ♖d4 48 ♗c6 ♔e5 49 ♔e3 f4+ 50 gxf4+ ♖xf4 51 h5 ♖h4 52 ♔d3 ♔f6 53 ♗e8 ♔e7 54 ♗c6 ♔d8 55 ♔c3 ♔c7 56 ♗e8 ♔b6 57 ♔d3 ♔c5**

58 ♔c3 ♔xd5 59 ♔d3 ♔e5 60 ♔e3 ♖f4 61 ♗b5 ♔f5 62 h6 ♖e4+ 63 ♔f3 ♖h4 64 h7 ♔f6 65 ♗d3 ♔g7 66 ♗e4 ♖h3+ 67 ♔e2 ♖h2+ 68 ♔e1 ♔f6 69 ♗d3 ♔e5 70 ♗g6 ♔f4 71 ♔f1 ♔e3 0-1.

30)

Ni Hua – Benjamin

USA-China Summit, Shanghai 2002

After **42...♖b3** White resigned. Fork, pin and skewer all play a part in the continuation 43 ♖xc6 ♘b4+ 44 ♔c4 ♖xc3+, by which Black nets a piece.

31)

Olivier – Manik

Mitropa Cup, Baden 1999

The game continued **16 ♘h6+!** (getting rid of the knight with gain of tempo; 16 ♘e7+? is wrong because 16...♘xe7 covers f5) **16...gxh6** (16...♔h8 17 ♘f7+) **17 ♖f5** (thanks to the pin, Black's queen is trapped) **17...♕xf5 18 exf5**.

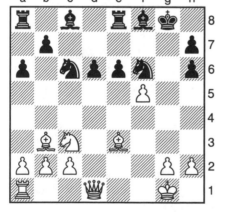

18...♔h8 (on top of the loss of material, Black's pawn-structure has been badly damaged so White wins easily) **19 fxe6 ♗xe6 20 ♕d2 ♗xb3 21 axb3 d5 22 ♖f1 d4 23 ♗xd4 ♘xd4 24 ♕xd4 ♗g7 25 ♖d1 h5 26 ♕f4 ♘g4 27 h3 ♗e5 28 ♕d2 ♘e3 29 ♖e1 ♘f5 30 ♘d5 ♗d4+ 31 ♔h2 h4 32 ♘e7 ♖xe7 33 ♖xe7** ♖d8 34 ♕g5 ♘xe7 35 ♕xe7 ♖c8 36 c3 ♗g7 37 ♕xb7 ♗e5+ 38 ♔g1 ♖b8 39 ♕e7 ♗g3 40 ♔f1 1-0.

32)

Anand – Nikolić

FIDE Knockout, Groningen 1997

The preliminary sacrifice **27 ♖xd7!** ♔xd7 pinned the knight so that White could trap Black's queen by **28 ♖b4**. 28...♕f5 29 g4 is hopeless for Black, so in desperation he gave up his queen by **28...♕xb4 29 ♗xb4 ♖hc8**. White finished efficiently: **30 ♗d6 ♖c4 31 ♘d2 ♖d4 32 c3 ♖d3 33 c4 ♖xd2 34 ♕xd2 bxc4 35 ♕xh6 1-0**.

33)

Kasimdzhanov – Smirin

Olympiad, Elista 1998

It seems impossible to trap the b7-knight, because it can safely retreat to a5. However, **20...♘xe2+** (not 20...♖fb8 first due to 21 ♗xf4) **21 ♕xe2 ♖fb8** pinpointed the key weakness of White's position: the undefended rook on b1.

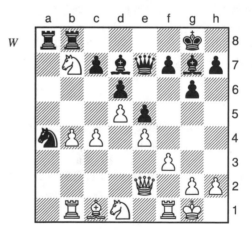

Since 22 ♘a5 ♖xa5 would cost White a piece for nothing, he tried **22 c5**, but after **22...dxc5 23 bxc5 ♘xc5 24 ♘xc5 ♖xb1 25 ♘xd7** White resigned without waiting for the decisive 25...♕xd7.

34)

Ibragimov – Yandemirov
Russian Ch, Elista 1997

White's pressure along the diagonal b2-g7 suggests some tactical ideas, and he won material by combining a fork with a discovered attack: **34 e5! ♕xe5 35 ♘f5+!**.

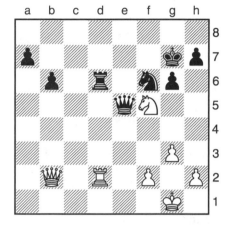

35...gxf5 (35...♕xf5 36 ♖xd6 is also hopeless for Black) **36 ♕xe5 ♖xd2 37 ♕xf5** (White has won a queen for a rook and a knight; Black fights on but without any real hope of saving the game) **37...♖d5 38 ♕e6 ♖d7 39 g4 ♖f7 40 f4 ♘g8 41 f5 ♘h6 42 h3 a5 43 ♕e5+ ♔f8 44 f6 ♖d7 45 ♕e6 ♖d1+ 46 ♔f2 ♘g8 47 g5 ♖d8 48 ♕xb6 ♖d7 49 ♕c5+ 1-0**.

35)

Schekachev – Lopushnoi
Russia Cup, Tomsk 1998

It hardly looks as though Black is doomed because of a weak back rank, but just see what happens: **20 ♘xd5!** and Black resigned! The main line runs 20...exd5 21 ♗xd6 ♖xe1 22 ♖xe1 ♗xd6 23 ♕xd6 and after 23...♕xd6 24 ♖e8+ Black does indeed get mated. Of course, Black could deviate at virtually any point in this line and play on a pawn down with a bad position, but apparently he just didn't feel like struggling on.

36)

Borovikov – Aleksandrov
Kramatorsk 2001

A long but forcing continuation led to a decisive gain of material: **30...♘f2+! 31 ♖xf2 ♖d1+ 32 ♗g1 ♖gxg1+** (not 32...♖dxg1+ 33 ♔h2, when Black has nothing) **33 ♔h2 ♖h1+ 34 ♔g3 ♖dg1+** (34...♖d3+ is equally good) **0-1**. After 35 ♖g2 ♖xg2+ 36 ♔xg2 ♖xh4 Black has an extra rook.

Solutions to Miscellaneous Exercises

1)

Vladimirov – Bacrot
Europe-Asia rapidplay, Batumi 2001

The simple move **31...♖e1+** gave Black a decisive material advantage. After **32 ♔h2** (or 32 ♔f2 ♖xd1 33 ♕xf6 ♕d4+, forcing the exchange of queens with a winning endgame) **32...♖xd1 33 ♕xf6** (the mating threats on g7 and f8 would be awkward except for the fact that Black can exchange queens) **33...♕d6+ 34 ♕xd6 ♖xd6** the ending is hopeless and White soon gave up: **35 ♔g3 ♖e6 36 ♔f2 ♔f7 37 ♗d2 c5 38 ♗c3 ♔e7 39 ♗d2 ♔d6 0-1**.

2)

Zhu Chen – Spassky
Veterans-Women, Marbella 1999

Black won with a combination of deflection and in-between move: **26...♕g6! 0-1**. 27 ♕xg6 ♖xd1+ 28 ♔h2 fxg6 and 27 ♕e2 ♖xd1+ 28 ♕xd1 ♕xe4 both cost White a rook.

3)

Dautov – Khuzman
Zonal tournament, Dresden 1998

White won with a combination based on opening the g-file: **25 ♕xf6!** and Black resigned, since mate is threatened on g7, while 25...gxf6 loses to 26 ♖g4+ ♔h8 27 ♗xf6#.

4)
Emms – Sutovsky
Harplinge 1998

After **37...♖e1+** White resigned as 38 ♔g2 ♖e2+ followed by ...♖xc2 wins his bishop.

5)
H. Olafsson – Rødgaard
Munkebo 1998

White has a forced mate in seven moves with the deflection **33 ♗h5+!**. After 33...♔f5 White mates by 34 ♕d6! (threatening 35 ♕f4#) 34...e5 35 f3 (threatening 36 g4+ ♔f4 37 ♕d2#) 35...♕d8 36 ♕xd8 e4 37 ♕d7+ ♔e5 38 f4#, while 33...♔g7 34 ♕xf7+ ♔h8 35 ♕xf6+ ♔g8 36 ♗f7+ ♔f8 37 ♗g6+ ♔g8 38 ♕f7+ ♔h8 39 ♕h7# only lasts one move longer. The game ended even more quickly after **33...♔xh5 34 ♕xf7+ ♔g4 35 ♕g6#**.

6)
I. Sokolov – Seirawan
Dutch Team Ch playoff, Enschede 2002

A preliminary sacrifice draws the black queen into position for a deadly skewer: **38 ♖xd7! ♕xd7 39 ♖c7** (the queen cannot move due to a possible mate on g7; Black must lose material) **39...♖ad8 40 ♖xd7 ♖xd7 41 ♗xf6 1-0**. Black is too far behind on material.

7)
Zelčić – Van Wely
Olympiad, Elista 1998

Black found a decisive combination utilizing a deflection and a fork: **32...♗xe4! 33 ♕xe4 d5** (now 34 ♕d3 c4 is a deadly fork, so White has to abandon the f5-rook) **34 ♕f3 ♕xf5 35 g3 ♕h3 36 ♖b7 ♗g5 37 ♘c6 ♗xh4 38 ♘xd8 ♖xd8 0-1**.

8)
Portisch – Hickl
Jakarta 1996

After **28 ♖h8+**, Black resigned at once since 28...♔xh8 29 ♘xf7+ followed by ♘xg5 leaves White well ahead on material.

9)
Marciano – Bricard
French Ch, Narbonne 1997

Black saved the position by **25...♗xg2!**. If White declines the bishop by 26 ♖hd1, for example, then after 26...♖fxf2 Black would even have some advantage; 27...♖f3+ is a threat and in addition the black rooks are ideally placed to gobble up White's queenside pawns. The game ended **26 ♔xg2 ½-½** since 26...♖exf2+ gives perpetual check with the rooks along the f-file.

10)
Plaskett – Pein
Southend 1999

A familiar pattern emerges after a few preliminary moves. White played **17 e5!** and Black resigned in anticipation of 17...fxe5 18 fxe5 ♗xe5 (Black must accept, or he loses his bishop) 19 ♖xe5 ♕xe5 (everything is in place for the idea we first saw in Bui Vinh-Frey on page 47) 20 ♖f8+ (once more this typical deflection strikes) 20...♖xf8 21 ♕xe5 and White, with queen and knight for two rooks and a pawn, has a decisive material advantage.

11)
Santo-Roman – Spassky
French Team Ch, Paris 2002

Here the winning ideas are fork and trapped piece. Black continued **35...♘d5!** and White resigned. The bishop cannot move so as to maintain its defence of the a1-rook, while after 36 ♖xa2 ♘xc3 White loses a whole rook and so ends up a piece down.

12)
Kengis – Godena
European Team Ch, Leon 2001

White won a piece with the back-rank combination **37 ♕xc5!**. Since 37...♕xc5 38 ♖d8+ ♕c8 39 ♖xc8# is impossible, Black was reduced to **37...♕b8**, but after **38 ♖xe5 fxe5** he resigned.

13)

McNab – Plaskett
Southend 1999

A combination of deflection and back-rank mate ensured Black's downfall: **42 ♕xe6+!** and Black resigned, as mate is forced after 42...♗xe6 43 ♗xe6+ ♔h8 44 ♖xf8+ ♖xf8 45 ♖xf8#.

14)

Lautner – Lendwai
Aschach 1997

White resigned after **38...♕d1+!** as there is a back-rank mate next move.

15)

Kacheishvili – Fedorov
European Team Ch, Leon 2001

Black must act quickly, since if White can exchange off the e5-bishop then the result will probably be a draw. The winning move is **52...♖d2+!**, since after 53 ♔xd2 ♗xa1 54 ♘b4 ♗c3+! Black promotes the pawn. White therefore resigned.

16)

Zakharevich – Bigaliev
Russia Cup, Krasnodar 1997

White capitalized on his d-pawn by **36 ♗h4! ♖xd6** (if the rook moves anywhere else, White just plays d7) **37 ♗e7+ ♔g8 38 ♗xd6 ♘xd6** (White's material advantage is decisive since Black will sooner or later lose his b-pawn) **39 ♖c6 ♘e4 40 ♔f3 ♘d2+ 41 ♔e2 ♘e4 42 ♔e3 ♘f6 43 h3 ♔f7 44 ♖c5 1-0**.

17)

Banas – Ruckschloss
Slovakian Ch, Prievidza 1998

White won with a combination involving an in-between move: **8 ♘xe5!** and now the key line runs 8...♗xe2 9 ♕a4+ (this in-between check decides matters as Black has no decent interposition) 9...♘c6 10 dxc6 and Black faces heavy material loss. The game continued 8...♗d7 9 ♘xd7 ♕xd7 10 ♗g4 (Black is not only a pawn down, but in addition his light squares have been irreparably weakened) **10...♕c7 11 ♕a4+ ♔d8 12 ♘b5 ♕b6 13 ♘xd6! 1-0**. The neat finish is based on the line 13...♕xd6 14 ♗f4, when Black must lose his queen to avoid mate on d7.

18)

Anastasian – Estremera Panos
Linares open 2000

White's queen has ventured further into enemy territory than is wise and Black found a neat combination to trap it: **22...♖xb4! 23 axb4 ♖e7 24 ♕b8** (giving up the queen by 24 ♖xa6 ♖xa7 25 ♖xa7 ♕d6 is hopeless) **24...♘fd7 25 ♕a7** (the queen must return as 25 ♕d6 ♖e6 traps it immediately) **25...♘e5** (the knight is transferred to c6 with gain of time) **0-1**. After 26 ♕b8 ♘c6 there is no way out.

19)

Hutchinson – S. Williams
British Ch, Torquay 2002

This is based on the familiar pattern of Bui Vinh-Frey on page 47, but a preliminary exchange is necessary to set it up. The game continued **24...♘xd4 25 ♕xd4** (now we have the typical set-up of a queen defended by a rook from the first rank) **25...♖e1+** (this deflection doesn't have an instantly catastrophic effect, but it is still enough to win) **26 ♔f2 ♖xd1 27 ♕xd1 ♕xb2+ 28 ♕e2 ♕xa3** (Black is two pawns up without compensation and won quickly) **29 ♕c2 g6 30 h4 b6 31 ♔g3 ♕c5 32 ♕e2 ♕d6+ 33 ♔f2 a5 34 g4 ♕h2+ 35 ♔e1 ♕xe2+ 0-1**.

20)

Morozevich – J. Polgar
Rapidplay, Frankfurt 1999

The f7-c4 line-up is suggestive, and indeed Black was able to win White's queen by **43...♘f3+** (setting up a discovered attack) **44 gxf3 ♖d1+ 45 ♕f1 ♖xf1+ 46 ♔xf1 ♕c4+**

(winning the bishop with a fork and so wrapping the game up) **47 ♔g2 ♕xf4 48 a4 ♔h6 0-1**.

21)
Leko – Adams
Dortmund 1999

White struck with a combination based on an h-file pin: **28 ♗xh6! ♕xh6** (28...gxh6 29 ♘g5+ ♔h8 30 ♖e6 is winning for White; for example, 30...♗xf2+ 31 ♔f1 ♘e3+ 32 ♔e2 and Black has no reasonable check) **29 ♕g5!** (now Black loses his queen) **29...a4 30 ♖e6 1-0**.

22)
Murey – Kantsler
Israeli Team Ch, Ramat Aviv 2000

Black won by **36...c6**, driving the rook away from the defence of f5. White must surrender the rook to avoid mate, so he resigned.

23)
Hellsten – San Segundo
European Team Ch, Pula 1997

White spotted the possibility of a knight fork on f4 and continued **49 ♖xd5!**. Now 49...♔xd5 50 ♘f4+ followed by 51 ♘xh3 is hopeless for Black, while 49...♖h1+ 50 ♔g2 doesn't help, so he played **49...♖xa3**, hoping to eliminate White's last pawn (the ending of ♖+♘ vs ♖ without pawns is drawn). However, White was able to keep his pawn and won after **50 ♖d4+ ♔b5 51 ♔e2 ♖c3** (51...♖b3 52 ♘c7+ ♔c6 53 ♖c4+ also wins for White) **52 ♘c5 ♖c2+ 53 ♔e3 ♖h2 54 ♘d3 1-0**.

24)
Epishin – Korobov
European Ch, Ohrid 2001

Black forced mate in four with a combination based on line-opening and square-clearance: **34...♖h4+!** and White resigned in view of 35 gxh4 (or 35 ♔g5 h6+ 36 ♔xg6 ♕h7#) 35...♕g2+ 36 ♔h5 (now Black could

mate by ...♕g6# if only his knight were not blocking that square) 36...♘f4+! (vacating g6 with gain of tempo) 37 ♖xf4 ♕g6#.

25)
Fedorov – Yusupov
European Team Ch, Batumi 1999

Black's pieces on f5 and h5 are set up for a possible pawn fork, but Black's h4-pawn stands ready to capture White's g-pawn *en passant* if it should advance to g4. However, this doesn't matter because a second fork then arises on g3: **21 g4! ♗xg4** (Black prefers to give up a piece for two pawns rather than lose the exchange after 21...hxg3 22 ♘xg3 g6 23 ♘xh5) **22 ♘xg4 ♘xg4 23 hxg4 ♖g6 24 b3 ♖xg4+ 25 ♔h2 a4 26 ♘c3 axb3 27 axb3** (Black would lose in the long run in any case, but his next move shortens the process) **27...c6? 28 d6 ♖d4 29 ♘d5!** (a neat tactical point; after 29...cxd5 30 d7 White threatens 31 d8♕# and 31 ♖e8#) **29...♖d2+ 30 ♔h1 1-0**. Black must lose further material.

26)
Wells – Rowson
London 1997

After the natural sequence of captures 28...♖xd7 29 ♗xd7 ♕xd7, White plays 30 ♕xg6+ and Black's pawns fall one after the other. In the game Black found a neat draw: **28...♕b6+!** (28...♖xd7 29 ♗xd7 ♕b6+ also works) **29 ♔g2 ♖xd7 30 ♗xd7 ♕b2+ 31 ♔f1 ♕c1+ ½-½**. With White's pieces so far away, there is no escape from Black's checks.

27)
Tkachev – Oll
FIDE Knockout, Groningen 1997

White played **29 ♗xe5** and Black resigned. If 29...♘xe5, then 30 ♘f6+ is an immediate fork, while after 29...♖xe5 30 ♘f6+ followed by 31 ♘d7 the fork is delayed by only one move. In either case Black suffers a fatal loss of material.

28)

Gomez Esteban – V. Georgiev
Elgoibar 1998

White won Black's queen with the discovered attack **28 ♖xg6+ fxg6 29 ♕xf2**. Black struggled on a few moves before resigning.

29)

Hübner – Ivanchuk
Dortmund 1997

Black has sacrificed a piece to reach this position and he now delivered the knock-out blow **35...♘f4!**.

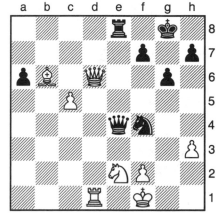

This threatens mates by 36...♕h1+ 37 ♘g1 ♕g2# and 36...♕g2+ 37 ♔e1 ♖xe2#) **36 ♕xf4** (36 ♘xf4 ♕h1#) **36...♕xe2+ 37 ♔g2 ♕xd1** (Black is now the exchange and a pawn up, more than enough for an easy win) **38 ♕c4 ♕e2 39 ♕a4 ♕e4+ 40 ♕xe4 ♖xe4 41 c6 ♖c4 42 c7 ♔f8 0-1**.

30)

Wiertzema – Anderberg
Düsseldorf 1996

White won by means of a line-closing combination: **34 ♖b5! axb5** (now 35 b7? fails to 35...bxc4, but there is a finesse) **35 c5!** (surprisingly, Black is unable to stop the b-pawn) **35...dxc5 36 b7 ♖xe3 37 ♔f2 ♖b3 38 b8♕** (now White wins easily with his material

advantage) **38...c4 39 ♕xe5 b4 40 ♕e6+ ♔g7 41 ♕xe7+** (Black's pawns fall one by one) **41...♔h8 42 ♕f6+ ♔h7 43 ♕f7+ ♔h8 44 ♕xc4 ♖b2+ 45 ♔e3 1-0**.

31)

Vidarsson – Stefansson
Icelandic Ch, Seltjarnarnes 2002

White's bishop is pinned and this so restricts his mobility that after **28...♗c3!** he cannot meet the threat of 29...♖d2; for example, 29 ♖d1 loses to 29...♗xb2+ 30 ♕xb2 ♖xd1+, winning White's queen. He therefore resigned.

32)

Gallagher – Efimov
European Team Ch, Pula 1997

Black won by removing the piece that prevents a deadly check on f4: **36...♖xe6! 37 ♕xe6** (there is no way out; 37 ♖xe6 is also met by 37...♗f4+ while the tricky 37 ♖f8+, hoping for 37...♗xf8?? 38 ♕xf8#, loses to 37...♔g7! 38 ♕b8 ♖b6, when Black will win more material) **37...♗f4+** and White resigned, since the only way to avoid mate is to play 38 ♖xf4, giving up the queen.

33)

Groberman – Pixton
USA Ch, Seattle 2002

The game continued **37...♖xf1** (deflecting the white rook from protecting the c2-pawn) **38 ♖xf1 ♕xc2+** (Black's queen joins in the attack with deadly effect) **39 ♔e3 ♕d3+ 40 ♔f4 ♕f5+** (Black repeats moves before taking the white rook) **41 ♔e3 ♕d3+ 42 ♔f4 ♕xf1** (Black is a piece up and won quickly) **43 ♔xg4 ♗c2 44 ♔f4 ♕c1+ 45 ♔e5 ♕h6! 46 ♕g8 ♔e7 0-1**.

34)

Iordachescu – Milu
Ciocaltea memorial, Bucharest 1998

After **39 ♖d8** Black resigned because he loses his queen for a rook.

35)

Sedlak – Sadvakasov
Subotica 2000

Black won material with a combination of fork and deflection: **37...♗d2+** (forking king and rook, so White must take the bishop even though this loses the exchange) **38 ♘xd2 ♖xc1 39 ♖a3 ♖e1+ 40 ♔d3 ♗e2+ 41 ♔e3 ♗d1+ 0-1**. 42 ♔d3 ♗c2# is mate, while 42 ♔f2 ♖e2+ costs White more material.

36)

Aleksandrov – Becerra Rivero
FIDE Knockout, Las Vegas 1999

White played **29 ♖xc3** and Black resigned since he is losing a piece (after 29...dxc3 30 ♖xd5 c2 White can stop the pawn with 31 ♖c5).

37)

Benjamin – de Firmian
USA Ch, Denver 1998

At the moment one cannot see a skewer, but Black set one up with a spectacular queen sacrifice: **33...♕xf1+! 34 ♔xf1 ♖d1+ 35 ♔e2 ♖e1+**.

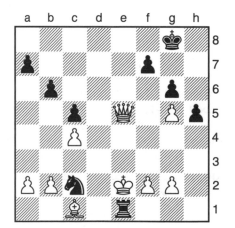

After **36 ♔d2 ♖xe5 37 ♔xc2 ♖e2+** White resigned, since he has not only lost the exchange, but also stands to lose most of his kingside pawns as well.

38)

Voiska – Zawadzka
European Women's Ch, Varna 2002

After **27 ♖xe8+** Black resigned, because 27...♕xe8 28 ♕xf6 leaves White a clear piece up.

39)

Doroshkevich – Shishkov
Chigorin memorial, St Petersburg 1999

Black's weak back rank stands out as a weakness. White exploited this by **30 ♕b4!** and Black resigned as the attacks on c4 and b8 will cost him a piece.

40)

Miles – Nataf
Capablanca memorial, Havana 2001

After **19 ♘g3** Black's queen is trapped (19...b5 20 ♕e4 doesn't help) and so he resigned. This was probably a case of inattention because, with f5 and g4 available, it didn't appear likely that the queen would suddenly run out of squares.

41)

M. Gurevich – Van der Sterren
Dutch Team Ch playoff, Enschede 2002

Black is attacking both b4 and e7, but despite this White managed to win material: **40 f6!**. Now 40...♘xf6 costs the knight after 41 ♖d6+, while 40...♘xb4 41 ♖d8 (not 41 f7?? because 41...♖xe7+ is check) wins too much material.

42)

Mikhalchishin – Schmittdiel
Dortmund 1999

White won with the promotion combination **46 ♖f8!** (not 46 ♖xh7+? ♕xh7 47 e8♕+ ♖xe8 48 ♕xe8+ ♕g8 with a draw) **46...♘xf8** (46...♕xf8+ 47 exf8♕+ ♘xf8 48 ♕f6+, winning the rook, is hopeless for Black) **47 ♕f6+ 1-0**. It is surprising that Black resigned here as there is one final finesse: 47...♔h7 48 exf8♘+! and Black must give up his queen, but not 48 exf8♕? ♕c4+, when Black delivers perpetual check.

43)

P.H. Nielsen – Holst
Års 1999

White won with a combination of pin and deflection. After **40 ♖d7+!** Black cannot take the rook with his bishop because it is pinned. Thus he has to move his king, but after 40...♔xd7 the king no longer guards the queen and White can play 41 ♕xb6. Therefore Black resigned.

44)

Kogan – Radziewicz
Koszalin 1999

White continued **24 ♗xf5** and Black resigned. His queen is attacked, so he must reply 24...♕xf5, but then 25 ♖f3 wins material since Black cannot move his queen without losing the f6-rook.

45)

Akopian – Gelfand
Groningen 1996

The game continued **28 ♖xb6 ♖xc4 29 ♖xb7? ♖d4** and ended in a draw, but in the middle of this line White missed the chance to win a piece by the in-between move 29 ♖xf6!.

46)

Borge – Mortensen
Danish Ch, Århus 1999

Black ensured the promotion of his f-pawn by the ingenious move **62...♘d3!** (62...♔e2 63 ♖c1 f1♕+ 64 ♖xf1 ♔xf1 wins the rook, but White can capture Black's last pawn after 65 a6 ♘c6 66 ♔g4 d5 67 ♔f4 ♔e2 68 a7 ♘xa7 69 ♔e5). The knight move controls c1, so the rook can't get back to stop the pawn. Therefore White has nothing better than 63 ♖xd3+ ♔e2 64 ♖xd6 (the pawn cannot be stopped), but after 64...f1♕+ 65 ♔g3 ♕f3+, followed by 66...♕f4+, Black wins the rook. White resigned immediately.

47)

Braun – Rabiega
German Ch, Altenkirchen 2001

The g6-bishop has to prevent ♖xh5#, so the deflection **40 f5** was deadly. Black resigned since he must lose a piece or be mated.

48)

Ovod – Shalimov
Chigorin memorial, St Petersburg 2002

Black's two connected passed pawns look unstoppable, but stalemate came to White's rescue: **72 ♗xc3!** (72 e8♕ ♗xe8 73 ♗xc3 also works; Black can refuse the bishop, but the opposite-coloured bishop ending is a simple draw) **72...♔xc3 73 e8♕ ♗xe8** stalemate.

49)

Siegel – Vallejo Pons
Capablanca memorial, Havana 1998

White is threatening mate on g7, but that didn't make the slightest difference after **33...♘d5**, both defending against the mate and forking White's queen and rook. Faced with a decisive material loss, White resigned.

50)

D. Gurevich – I. Ivanov
USA Ch, Denver 1998

White has a potential knight fork on e4, but at the moment his bishop is obstructing this square. The game continued **25 ♗xh7+!** (clearing e4 with a forcing move which gives Black no time to avoid the fork) **25...♔xh7 26 ♘e4 ♕xd5 27 ♘xc3** and White was the exchange up without compensation, an advantage which proved sufficient to win.

51)

Rublevsky – Nguyen Anh Dung
FIDE Knockout, Moscow 2001

A deflection of the f2-pawn sets the stage for the decisive fork: **30...♖xe3 31 ♕g5** (31 fxe3 ♗g3 followed by 32...♗xe1 is the main idea, but it leaves Black a piece up for nothing) **31...♖e5 32 ♕xg6 ♘ce4** (with only one pawn for the piece, White's position is hopeless) **33 ♘xe4 ♖xe4 34 ♔f1 ♗b4 35 ♖d1 ♕h2 36 f3 ♗c5 37 ♔e1 ♕g1+ 38 ♔d2 ♕e3+ 0-1**.

52)
R. Burnett – Hoang Thanh Trang
Budapest 2000

Rather surprisingly, it is the undefended rook on b1 which is the target of Black's combination. The game continued **25...♖xh3!** (playing 25...♘xe3+ and only then 26...♖xh3 is also good) **26 ♖xh3 ♖xh3 27 ♗xg5** (the main line is 27 ♔xh3 ♕h7+ 28 ♔g2 ♘xe3+ 29 ♕xe3 ♕xb1 and the discovered attack along the h7-b1 diagonal leaves Black a piece up) **27...♖h7 28 ♘f6** (28 ♗xe7 ♕xg4 is also hopeless for White) **28...♗xf6 29 ♗xf6 ♕g6** and Black is a piece up for just one pawn. White fought on but eventually had to resign.

53)
Vaïsser – Tkachev
Cannes 2000

The g3-pawn is pinned by Black's queen so he was able to win material and the game by **39...♖xf4+ 40 ♕xf4 gxf4 0-1**.

54)
Seul – Mainka
Essen 2000

36...♘d3 forks bishop and rook, and wins a piece. White therefore resigned.

55)
Alterman – Avrukh
Tel Aviv 1999

The deflection **34...♕xf4!** won a piece for nothing, since 35 exf4 allows mate in two by 35...♗d4+ 36 ♖e3 ♗xe3#. White resigned.

56)
Bastian – Lobron
German Ch, Altenkirchen 2001

After **30...♖xf2** White resigned, since 31 ♕xf2 ♗d4 32 ♖f1 ♗xf2+ 33 ♖xf2 leaves

Black with the decisive material advantage of queen and pawn for rook and bishop.

57)
Simutowe – Sarkar
New York 2001

White won by **34 ♖xf7+**, removing the guard of the key g6-square. It is mate after 34...♔xf7 35 ♕g6# or 34...♖xf7 35 ♕g6+ followed by 36 ♕g8#, so Black resigned.

58)
Postny – Stryjecki
European Junior Ch, Patras 2001

White won with a spectacular combination based on discovered attack combined with back-rank mate: **47 ♖xc7! ♖d8** (after 47...♖xc7 48 ♘g4! White attacks the queen and threatens mate by ♕h8+; then 48...♕f4 49 ♕h8+ ♖c8 50 ♕xc8+ ♕b8 51 ♕xb8+ leaves White two pieces up) **48 ♖d7 1-0**. Black is two pieces down and White wins easily with a direct attack based on b5.

59)
Seirawan – Adams
Match (game 1), Bermuda 1999

After **39...♔g7** there was no escape for White's rook. The finish was **40 ♖xf6 ♔xf6 41 h4 b5 0-1**.

60)
Stohl – Nikolaidis
European Team Ch, Pula 1997

The undefended d5-rook is a tactical weakness which White exploited by **22 ♗xa7!**. After **22...♖xa7** (Black cannot even escape with the loss of a pawn by 22...♕b7, because 23 ♗f3 pins the d5-rook and wins more material) **23 ♖xd5** White had won the exchange and the game concluded **23...e6 24 b6** (pushing the passed pawn is even simpler than 24 ♖d2) **24...♖xa2 25 ♖b5 d5 26 b7 ♘d6 27 ♕g3! e5 28 ♖b6 ♖a7 29 ♗a6 ♘xb7 30 ♕b3 ♖xa6 31 ♖xa6 ♕c7 32 ♕xd5 ♘d8 33 ♖a8 1-0**.

61)

Hulak – Bologan

European Ch, Ohrid 2001

White set up a fork on f6 with the preliminary sacrifice **23 ℤxh5**. After **23...♘xg5** (the alternative 23...ℤxh5 24 ♘f6 followed by ♘xh5 is also hopeless for Black) **24 ℤxh8 ℤxh8 25 fxg5 ♗xd5 26 cxd5** Black was a piece down and lost in due course.

62)

Hraček – Alterman

European Team Ch, Pula 1997

Black won with an unusual type of back-rank combination: **39...♕xf4!**.

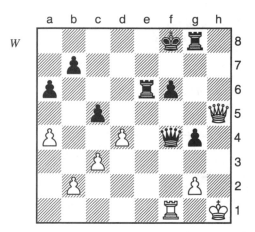

White resigned because 40 ℤxf4 allows Black to mate by 40...ℤe1+ 41 ♔h2 g3+ 42 ♔h3 ℤh1#.

63)

Fedorowicz – Shliperman

New York 1999

Black, who has just played **30...ℤe5-e4?**, resigned without waiting for White to reply 31 ♕xe4, exploiting the d-file pin.

64)

I. Sokolov – Magai

Olympiad, Elista 1998

This is another case of an adventurous queen being punished for a lone sortie into enemy territory. At present the queen can retreat to h3, but Black cut off this escape-route by **24...ℤf5!**, when there is no real defence to the threats of 25...♘f4 and 25...♘g7. The game concluded **25 ♘e4 ♘f4 26 ♕xd6 ℤxd6 27 ♘xd6 ℤf8 28 ℤbd1 ♕d7 29 h3 ♘xh3+ 0-1**. White resigned as after 30 gxh3 ♕xh3 followed by ...♗f4 Black has a decisive attack.

65)

Swathi – Hutchinson

British Ch, Torquay 2002

White won a piece by **32 ℤxb6+! ♔xb6 33 ♘c8+ ♔c7 34 ♘xe7**. Black has no compensation and gave up after **34...♘xh5 35 ♘f5 ♘f4 36 ♘xe5 ♘xg2 37 ♘xg7 ♘f4 38 ♔d2 ♔d6 39 ♘xf7+ ♔e7 40 ♘xh6 ♔f6 41 ♘e8+ ♔e7 42 ♘c7 1-0**.

66)

Loch – Rohrer

Germany (Oberliga) 1991/2

How can Black make use of his advanced a2-pawn? After 29...a1♕, White replies 30 ♕xb5 and Black is much worse. 29...♕xb4+ is also ineffective, since after 30 ♔xa2 White is a pawn up and does not face any immediate danger. The winning move is the surprising **29...a1♘+!**. By delivering check, Black does not give White the time to take on b5. 30 ℤxa1 is impossible as White's queen is left undefended, so there is nothing better than 30 ♔a2 ♕xd3 31 ℤxd3 ♘c2, when Black is a piece up with an easy win in prospect. White therefore resigned.

Index of Players

Numbers refer to pages. **Bold** text indicates that the player had White.